Paul Gasque's *Daybreak—Awakened to the Light of Christ* is an extraordinary take on how our hearts slowly respond to the whispers of the Lord speaking over us and into our lives. In this book, Paul reflects on his own ocean-side spiritual awakening, when through an encounter with Jesus, his eyes were suddenly opened to the importance of not only loving others but allowing their agape love to change our own hearts and lives, as well. Paul is a remarkable writer and Christian leaders whose work breathes love, guidance, insight and crucial Spirit wisdom, even for the most faithful among us. It's a must-read for anyone taking a next step with Jesus.

—Jessica Brodie (JessicaBrodie.com) is a Christian journalist, author, editor, blogger, and writing coach who runs the *South Carolina United Methodist Advocate*, the oldest newspaper in Methodism. Her novel, *The Memory Garden*, won the American Christian Fiction Writers' 2018 Genesis Contest. She has won hundreds of writing awards, and the newspaper she edits has won 113 awards under her leadership.

Daybreak

Awakened to the Light of Christ

Paul Gasque

WESTBOW
PRESS®
A DIVISION OF THOMAS NELSON
& ZONDERVAN

WestBow Press books may be ordered through booksellers or by contacting:

WestBow Press
A Division of Thomas Nelson & Zondervan
1663 Liberty Drive
Bloomington, IN 47403
www.westbowpress.com
1 (866) 928-1240

ISBN: 978-1-9736-7002-5 (sc)
ISBN: 978-1-9736-7001-8 (hc)
ISBN: 978-1-9736-7003-2 (e)

Library of Congress Control Number: 2019910233

Print information available on the last page.

WestBow Press rev. date: 08/27/2019

DEDICATION

To my Mom, Mary Elizabeth Gasque, who by her willingness to raise and care for more than her own biological children, taught me by godly example the virtues of feeding and tending those whom God puts in one's life. May this book be my gift to honor her memory and that her compassionate spirit might live in and through me.

EPIGRAPH

For unless light should shine on man in his dark state, he could never be gathered out of it; but he that is turned to the light, and followeth it, cannot abide in the darkness....But of what nature is this light, which shineth in man in his dark state? It is of a living nature; it is light which flows from life; it is light which hath life in it; it is the life of our Lord Jesus Christ.

Isaac Penington
English Quaker
1616-1679

CONTENTS

PREFACE

A dear, elderly lady from one of the churches I once served used to say to me, "Paul, tell me another story about your Papa." I would hear this every time I visited with her at the retirement home where she resided at the time. The humorous stories I had told her on previous visits had so entertained her that she wanted to hear another one with each ensuing visit. I don't know who enjoyed it more – she, or me watching her laugh until tears ran down her cheeks.

"You know why I can laugh so much about those stories, Paul?"

"Why is that?" I would ask.

"Because I am just like your Papa," she would say. And again she would break out into laughter.

Stories: these comprise our lives. What is it that gives meaning to our stories that make us both laugh and even cry?

My wife, Laura, and I enjoy the early morning hours of each day reading and meditating on scripture, praying, and immersing ourselves in devotional writings. One of my favorite spiritual disciplines is journaling – writing my personal thoughts and reflections on passages of scripture. I find it especially helpful to go back to a thought I wrote days or weeks earlier to consider how I might be living those thoughts now. She and I guard this time jealously not wanting anything to interfere with what has become the part of our day that we look so forward to. There are times when we both sit at the kitchen table in silence and thoughtful reflection. And then there are times when we retreat to separate rooms in the house for our respective solitude.

We are now in our retirement years with my having retired from law enforcement 20 years ago and from pastoral ministry almost seven years ago. Laura is in her seventh year of retirement from the local school system, having also served nine years in pastoral ministry. While our devotional times bring joy, introspection, and spiritual challenges to our lives, there are those other times when we find ourselves looking across the table at one another thinking *What now?* Where do our lives take us now? What might God's purpose be for us at this stage of our lives? Laura has brought this up with me on more than one occasion. I must admit I have not always been as faithful as I should be in giving this my careful and prayerful consideration.

One day Laura told me that she felt God might be calling me to write. Yes, I have learned over the years that Laura possesses a keen sense of discernment. Several years ago, on some of the mornings before she left for school, Laura would notice how I would sit at the kitchen table recording my thoughts on Scripture. One day she said to me, "Why don't you think about putting your thoughts into a book." I had never considered this, not even knowing where to start on such an endeavor. But her suggestion and encouragement were instrumental in my eventually writing a devotional book entitled *Lifting the Veil* (Westbow Press), my first venture into publishing. Here we are again – another long, arduous, and yet fulfilling journey in writing.

We all have experiences in life that return to our thoughts. Some may be more recent and others from earlier years. But each event has played a critical role in God's shaping of our lives. Unfortunately, many inspiring life stories are never told or shared. First, one might feel that her or his life experience is not or was not that important. Secondly, others might feel the event is far too personal to share. Thirdly, there are many who dismiss such times as though this is just the way life is. Whatever the case might be, my firm conviction is that giving voice to such events might bring hope and meaning to others in their own spiritual understanding for their lives.

I found the publication process tedious and agonizingly slow at times. In the weeks following the submission of my manuscript to Beth Williams, my first-draft editor, additional thoughts came to mind that I had not mentioned previously. Some, I believe, might have enhanced the overall message I sought to convey. Still others have drifted from my mind like the dissipation of a morning fog. Over time, there were times of self doubt, wanting to give up, to move on to other pursuits, only to return to my writing station, sensing that something more needed to be said.

One instance in particular was my frustration in locating Heike Jürrens, a subject in one of the stories. Heike was a young German student visiting in America in 1998. A wallet belonging to her was found on an exit ramp in Florence, South Carolina in June. Through the efforts and cooperation of concerned citizens, agencies and organizations unknown to one another, Heike's wallet was eventually returned to her. This story is compelling for the spiritual message it conveys. God uses people we least expect to find us when we are spiritually lost on a wayward path as that wallet was that day. Our life then becomes a journey back to the one true God to whom we belong.

I felt it necessary to communicate with Heike about my using her experience in America 20 years ago. I tried diligently to locate her by mail from a twenty-year-old home address, by telephoning a school in Germany that she once attended, and by contacting her family. All efforts were fruitless. I had even communicated with a German friend of ours in Virginia for help in contacting Heike by telephone. My impatience and discouragement had led me to pray that God would enable me to locate Heike in some way.

Months later as I was about to abandon my efforts, I made one more attempt to locate Heike – social media, which I probably should have done at the outset. And behold, here she was! I sent her a message from her profile, but heard nothing for a couple of days. As my excitement waned, I wondered if my message had gotten through to her. Two days later, she responded, with her own joy of having heard from me after all these years.

So, why do I share this now? Having finally contacted Heike

was the affirmation I needed to press on with my writing. I felt that, without question, this was answered prayer and if writing is my life purpose, if God is calling me to write, then I must write. What I have undertaken is simply to do what others can also do. We all have stories to tell of the awesome work God has done in our lives regardless of who we are. The process of opening personal segments of one's life to others is challenging but also therapeutic. This vulnerability leads to a spirit of honesty and openness when listening to the heartaches and struggles of those to whom God might have called us. How grateful I am for the people God has put in my life over the years – far too many to include in one work and others that I, unfortunately, may have forgotten about. I chose these for the impact they had in God's continuous work of shaping me and granting me the discernment to see Christ in those who come my way in the future. To God be the Glory.

ACKNOWLEDGMENTS

I wish to express my heartfelt appreciation to the many people who made this book possible. Their kindness in allowing me to use their stories and the story we shared together will always be a cherished memory of our friendship and a witness to how God brings people together to teach valuable faith lessons. I especially want to thank Beth Williams who graciously agreed to read and edit my initial draft. Her literary expertise and honest criticism served as a valuable teaching tool that will hopefully enhance my future writing skills. To my friends David Watson, Michael Bethea, Michael and Linda Donnell, Roger and Nancy Paxton, Tommy Coleman, Michael Roberts, my brother-in-law, and his wife Sandra and son Clay; and to Dottie Cronise, a former co-worker of mine at the South Carolina Law Enforcement Division, I thank you. Also contributing were the families of Willie Nettles (Pearl Nettles, Sandra Catlett, and Leeanne Rogers), Eloise Smith, and Iva Lee Pate. I also thank my daughter, Dr. Lauren Kuykendall, who rescued me in the formatting process that often befalls the aged and technologically ignorant like myself. I am also grateful to Heike Jürrens for allowing me to use her letter and beautiful art work sent to me in 1998 in appreciation for the people who worked tirelessly to help her in a time of need. I would extend my gratitude to Christa LeClere for the help she rendered to me in trying to locate Heike by telephone in Germany. I am especially deeply grateful for and indebted to my wife Laura who told me on more than one occasion how she sensed that God's purpose for me at this stage of my life is to write. Her encouragement, especially in those times when I was tempted to give up the process, gave me the inspiration to continue. Most of all, I want to thank God for how He has worked in my life, for the patience He has demonstrated to me in those utterly weak moments, and for the faith lessons he has taught me, some of which are shared in this book.

INTRODUCTION

Over the weeks leading up to the writing of this book, our days in the small town of Latta, South Carolina, have been a mixture of evening thunderstorms and oppressive summer heat. Recent days, however, have afforded a pleasant respite from the heat, with early-morning temperatures in the high fifties to low sixties. This hint of fall in the air has a way of drawing me outside, opening my senses to a time of refreshment in God's Word and His marvelous creation.

This particular day in August began as almost every other day begins—taking our pet dog, Peppy, outside to do what I must do two or three times a night at my age. My wife, Laura, stepped out onto our driveway with Peppy on leash and made her way out onto the front yard. As I followed her moments later, she called my attention to a glorious array of pinks and coral oranges to the east. As if in a grand procession, a beautiful cloud formation was ushering in the light of another day. I stood for a moment and reflected on the beauty of it all and how it illumined my senses. Whether it is a sunrise or a sunset, such beauty leaves us both awestruck. I then walked into the house to gather up my Bible, devotional readings, prayer list, and notepad, returning outside to my favorite spot for quiet solitude in God's Word.

Early mornings have a reverent dimension that seems to enliven my senses to God's presence in my life. I am often joined in my readings by the occasional visit of a rabbit that has made its home in the azalea bushes close by. Blessings abound out among God's creation. The cool morning breezes that are rare for the summer season and the various birds lighting on the bird feeders hanging from the crepe myrtle trees along our driveway are a welcome addition to the new day. Words seem inadequate to capture the true essence of such glorious reminders of God's divine presence. But what comes to mind is *daybreak*.

The dawning of a new day had broken as Sandra Roberts rose from her bed and began her daily routine of having a quick breakfast, putting on makeup, getting dressed, and ensuring that she had everything needed for her work as the English department chair and teacher at Creek Bridge High School in Marion County, South Carolina. She woke her son, Clay, in time for him to also get ready. Clay rode with her every morning, since the satellite center for Florence/Darlington Technical College that he attended in the town of Mullins was along the route Sandra traveled each day. This convenient arrangement worked well for both of them.

Several miles away, Willie Nettles, a local self-employed woodworker, lay in his bed, hoping to get a few more minutes of sleep before beginning his day. It was Wednesday, October 24, 2012. Sandra and Clay left their home in Latta, traveling east on Highway 917 toward Mullins. A heavy fog blanketed the landscape that day, greatly reducing visibility. Minutes passed as Sandra drove slower than usual due to the hazardous driving conditions. Willie slept on. Sandra continued traveling east on Highway 917, enjoying the remaining few minutes she had with Clay before dropping him off in Mullins. Several miles from Latta, Sandra approached a curve, when suddenly—

A horrific crashing noise awakened Willie. "What was that?" He sensed that it was nearby. He quickly jumped out of bed and threw on some clothes. Willie and his sister, Sandy, who happened to be there with him, rushed outside to see what had happened. He could detect through the dense fog that a tragic automobile accident had occurred on the highway in front of his home, an apparent head-on collision. As he drew closer, Willie noticed the occupants of one of the vehicles. He rushed over to check on their condition. Sandra's car had veered off on the other side of the highway, resting partially in a ditch. She was struggling to breathe, fighting for her life. Clay was frantic, due to his mother's injuries and partially due to the fact that he had lost his glasses and his cell phone during the collision. Bleeding from where his head had hit the windshield and having difficulty seeing, Clay was trying to find his phone to call for help. Willie consoled them both, trying to help Sandra get her breath while at the same time trying to calm Clay. "Hold on," he begged them. "Help is on the way. Please, just hold on, hold on," he cried. Realizing that Clay could not find his phone, Willie offered to call Clay's father for him. Clay gave Willie his father's name and phone number. Willie recognized the name Michael Roberts, a friend Willie and Sandy had known from their high school years, although neither had ever met Michael's wife or son. Willie and Sandy stayed with Sandra and Clay until the local rescue squad arrived. The driver of the other vehicle died as a result of the accident.

Sandra barely hung on to life as the rescue vehicle rushed her to the nearest hospital. Because of the extensive nature of her injuries, Sandra was later transferred to a regional medical facility. During this time, she underwent seven surgeries. Once stable, she was placed in a private room for about two weeks. Clay was treated and released on the day of the accident. Sandra later underwent physical therapy for several months. Thankfully, they both lived to see another day.

On the day of the accident, people who never knew or had even met one another became "neighbors" in a spirit that brought glory to God. There may come times in your life and mine when God puts someone in our path whom we may or may not know, who may well be facing a *spiritual* life-and-death situation. The time and attention we give to that individual in their time of need may serve as the catalyst for the in-breaking of God's providential will in the life of that person. As time passes, you occasionally reflect on that experience from the past, thanking God for how He used you in such a time of need. But slowly, almost imperceptibly, you begin to sense that God had something profound to reveal to you through that situation. Deep within the recesses of your own spirit lies a hidden hopelessness desperately searching for a way out—a dark, seemingly unredeemed area of your being. You have been unable to name it. Could it be a sheer lack of purpose for and meaning to life? You long for a better day, a better situation, a better station in life. But when? As your heart becomes open to the Spirit of God moving in your life, there is a sound, the voice of a gentle whisper as if speaking to you from a remote distance, but drawing nearer and clearer, saying to you, "Hold on, hold on, for daybreak is coming. The light of Christ has not left you. Your new day has arrived."

CHAPTER 1

A New Day

I have heard it said at times that we never know what a day holds, but we know who holds it, or words to that effect. For most of us, our days are typically framed by our rising in the morning and our lying down at night. There are exceptions to this regimen for those whose employment and family responsibilities dictate schedules otherwise. Whatever challenges might come, whatever opportunities might abound, or whatever responsibilities might exist, they all fall within the few hours of one's day. There are occasional surprises, eager anticipations, and mundane tasks, all of which can leave you either fulfilled or frustrated—or a combination of both.

In a spiritual sense, what then might a *new* day represent in terms of one's eternal life—a day not marked by hours or governed by schedules, but a turning-point experience that sets the stage for a life journey guided by the Spirit of God; a time when one's life bears witness that he or she is not the same person today as in the past? In this context, the new day represents a new way of life in the unconditional love of God, demonstrated by the grace of Jesus Christ.

This new day came for me in the latter part of 1991. Although the specific date escapes me, the particular moment has left an indelible impression on me. I recall standing in the bedroom of our house, telling Laura that I felt a compelling urge to read the Bible in its entirety, something I had never done before. Although I had read portions of the Bible, I had never taken on a serious, disciplined study of God's Word. This spirit-led compulsion led to a pivotal season in my life throughout the following year.

Professionally, I was a supervisor with the South Carolina State Law Enforcement Division. Personally, I was happily married with two children, ages eight and six at the time. So, in January 1992, I began my first reading of the entire Bible. It was also in this same year that I took my first lay speaking class and had a couple of opportunities to bring the message during the worship service at my home church in Latta. I will never forget the fear and trepidation of standing before the congregation of my home church and proclaiming God's Word. Feelings of inadequacy and unworthiness seized me. I could just imagine some in the crowd thinking, *Who is this preaching today? Who does he think he is?* The feelings may have been more mine than those of anyone else. Notwithstanding the anxiety, I felt a sense of home as I stood in this totally unfamiliar place—the pulpit.

Up until then, I had been living a double life—torn between earthly pleasures and secular pursuits and where I felt God was leading me. I began to sense that I had a choice to make. For many years leading up to this, I was a social drinker. This was very much a part of my lifestyle—at social gatherings, tailgating at college football games, parties, outdoor grilling, whatever the occasion. As I became more involved in the life of the church, I recognized that drinking could very well be a problem for me if I did not come to terms with it. I resigned myself to drinking only on the weekends, refraining from it during the week. *Oh, how we rationalize our sins!* The urge was still there, tempting me to drink during the week. Some days I could refrain, but there were also times when I succumbed just to get me through. I found it difficult to give it up completely. All during this time, I was still reading and studying God's Word.

On the night of Christmas 1992, as I neared the completion of a yearlong reading of God's Word, the appointed time arrived. I was at the home of Laura's family as Christmas dinner was about to be served. My mother-in-law was stirring around, tending to the last-minute preparations. As I had a glass up to my mouth of what was to be my last scotch and water, it was as if a voice said to me, "Paul, what do you want, Me or alcohol?" It wasn't an audible voice but what I would call a sensing in my spirit—as if the Spirit of God was speaking to me. At this precise moment, every urge, every desire I ever had for alcohol vanished. What had become difficult for me was easy and entirely possible with God. It was at this point in my life that I believe—without question—God poured out His all-sufficient grace upon me and did for me what I could not do for myself. I came to understand and experience the awesome grace of God.

I have since come to realize how unworthy I am. It was here that I began to see life from a different perspective. I soon found myself making occasional trips to the hospital to visit with people from Latta or others I knew. My life had begun to take on many aspects that are associated with pastoral ministry. I have immersed myself in God's Word ever since. There is so much more that I could share with you about my personal struggles and the struggles I have shared vicariously with others. But, in all this, I have learned that people are more important than things, and serving as the hands and feet of Christ can be the greatest blessing anyone could ever have.

I have often looked back on that Christmas night and how I sensed the presence of God in what I would consider a miraculous way. But such reflection gives rise to a fundamental question, one that is still being asked of me today, even when my conscious mind is not attuned to it. Such a question can never be answered in a minute or an hour or any measured span of time. The only genuine answer comes from the heart.

CHAPTER 2

John 21: 1-19

Early on the morning of Friday, April 8, 2016, I awoke from sleep, rose from my bed, and made my way to the kitchen. Most of my days begin with my starting the coffeemaker and getting our dog and cat fed before settling in for my daily devotional time. I light a candle, which I find as a useful meditation tool, and set it nearby on the kitchen table. My practice is to start my time before daylight, so I also employ the use of a small battery-operated reading light. The presence of only candlelight and a small reading light enables me to focus on the passage I will be reading each morning.

Over the past several years, I have followed a disciplined approach of reading the four lectionary readings for each respective week, usually taking one on which to concentrate my study and reflections. Journaling my thoughts on scripture has become a welcome companion to my reflections—thoughts I return to occasionally. The reading for the upcoming Third Sunday of Easter was the Gospel of John, chapter 21, verses 1–19, which I had been reflecting on for a few days. In my meditations on this passage, I envisioned myself being on the shore with Jesus that day and His asking me, "Paul, do you love Me?" The more I read it, the more personally I experienced the passage as I began to consider and journal significant stages of my life. I share this passage of scripture with you now as the basis for the writing of this book.

> After these things Jesus showed himself again to the disciples by the Sea of Tiberias; and he showed himself in this way. Gathered there together were Simon Peter, Thomas called the Twin, Nathanael of Cana in Galilee, the sons of Zebedee, and two others of his disciples. Simon Peter said to them, "I am going fishing." They said to him, "We will go with you." They went out and got into the boat, but that night they caught nothing.
>
> Just after daybreak, Jesus stood on the beach; but the disciples did not know that it was Jesus. Jesus said to them, "Children, you have no fish, have you?" They answered him, "No." He said to them, "Cast the net to the right side of the boat, and you will find some." So they cast it, and now they were not able to haul it in because there were so many fish. That disciple whom Jesus loved said to Peter, "It is the Lord!" When Simon Peter heard that it was the Lord, he put on some clothes, for he was naked, and jumped into the sea. But the other disciples came in the boat, dragging the net full of fish, for they were not far from the land, only about a hundred yards off.
>
> When they had gone ashore, they saw a charcoal fire there, with fish on it, and bread. Jesus said to them, "Bring some of the fish that you have just caught." So Simon Peter went aboard and hauled the net ashore, full of large fish, a hundred fifty-three of them; and though there were so many, the net was not torn. Jesus said to them, "Come and have breakfast." Now none of the disciples dared to ask him, "Who are you?" because they knew it was the Lord. Jesus came and took the bread and gave it to them, and did the same with the fish. This was now the third time that Jesus appeared to the disciples after he was raised from the dead.
>
> When they had finished breakfast, Jesus said to Simon Peter, "Simon son of John, do you love me more than these?" He said to him, "Yes, Lord; you know

that I love you." Jesus said to him, "Feed my lambs." A second time he said to him, "Simon son of John, do you love me?" He said to him, "Yes, Lord; you know that I love you." Jesus said to him, "Tend my sheep." He said to him the third time, "Simon son of John, do you love me?" Peter felt hurt because he said to him the third time, "Do you love me?" And he said to him, "Lord, you know everything; you know that I love you." Jesus said to him, "Feed my sheep. Very truly, I tell you, when you were younger, you used to fasten your own belt and to go wherever you wished. But when you grow old, you will stretch out your hands, and someone else will fasten a belt around you and take you where you do not wish to go." (He said this to indicate the kind of death by which he would glorify God.) After this he said to him, "Follow me." (John 21:1–19, New Revised Standard Version).

CHAPTER 3

The Question: "Do You Love Me?"

Throughout our lives, we are confronted with questions, many of which we must answer yes or no. Often we qualify our response based on some inherent longing or desire or how we anticipate another person might react to our response. Our answers tend to say more about who we are than we sometimes realize.

As I meditated deeply on chapter 21 of John's gospel during that week in April 2016, I envisioned in my mind's eye my being there that day with Jesus and being asked the question. *What in my life might be the impetus for this question to be asked of me by my Lord? In what ways has my faithfulness and obedience fallen short of what Christ has called me to? How far could I go with this thought, and what might I learn from it?* The two of us are seated on a small pile of rocks not far from the shoreline. The oncoming waves gently break the silence as they roll in upon the rocky shore. A grove of trees and dense vegetation frame the narrow shoreline a short distance behind us. Jesus is seated with His legs crossed, gazing intently into a crackling fire that He had started earlier. I am seated perpendicular to His left, next to Him. We both seem to be momentarily immersed in our own private thoughts. *What might*

He be thinking? I wonder. The silence alone bears an unsettling anxiousness. Jesus looks slowly over at me and asks, "Paul, do you love Me?"

This is a question rarely asked. Perhaps it's spoken most often when meaningful or longstanding relationships appear in question. Those intense heartbreaking moments come when one spouse tells another, "I don't love you anymore. I want out of the marriage," especially when the one hearing those words had no idea that the other felt this way. Some of us may have had the misfortune of learning of the marriage of a couple we knew personally ending in this way. I sense that Jesus already knew my answer and has His own reason for asking. The fire crackles as I gather my thoughts to respond. Is it not true, I wonder, that the answer to such a question is better conveyed by the devotion, attention, and affection one shows to another that obviates the need for it ever to be asked? Without belaboring Jesus's reason for asking, I respond, "Why yes, Lord, You know that I love You." Having heard my answer, Jesus casts His eyes toward the sea, caught up in a moment of thoughtful reflection.

At the outset of Jesus's ministry, He called His first four disciples as He passed along the shore of the Sea of Galilee. Simon and Andrew were casting their net into the sea, and two brothers, James and John, were in their boat with their father, Zebedee, mending their nets when Jesus called them to follow Him. These four immediately left what they were doing to go with Jesus. We find this a bit difficult to grasp in the context of our own times, to just up and leave all we have known and worked for to set out on a life we know nothing about. What might have captivated them to leave so abruptly, to leave their livelihood and family? Scripture does not tell us any more than what Jesus urged them to do—to follow Him and He would make them fish for people. In that meager, tedious, mundane existence, these four must have caught a sense of purpose for their lives in following Jesus. Obviously, Jesus spoke in a context they could understand. But there must have been more; more that they were about to witness as they entered the synagogue in Capernaum where they had gone with Jesus on the Sabbath day.

Many who had gathered in the synagogue that day must have heard earlier of the teachings of this man from Nazareth. Among them sat a man possessed by an unclean spirit. Why was he there? Was he known to the others there? What was he seeking? Did he know Jesus would be teaching there that day? There he sat listening attentively as Jesus spoke and taught with words that were quite unlike those the people there that day had previously heard from the scribes. As Jesus continued to speak, the man grew restless. Suddenly, a loud shrieking scream interrupted the service. The others looked to where the voice had come from, startled by the disturbance. "What have you to do with us, Jesus of Nazareth? Have you come to destroy us? I know who you are, the Holy One of God," came a shout from the man (Mark 1:24, NRSV). The authority of Jesus's teaching had riled up the unclean spirit in the man. "But Jesus rebuked him, saying, 'Be silent, and come out of him!' And the unclean spirit, convulsing him and crying with a loud voice, came out of him" (v. 25b–26). For several minutes, all eyes were on the writhing of the man as he shook uncontrollably, the unclean spirit responding to the power and authority of Jesus. The spectacle astounded and amazed the people, leading them to ask, "What is this? A new teaching—with authority" (v. 27b)! I can only imagine how, moments later, the man lay motionless on the floor, sweating profusely and breathing heavily. Many in the crowd looked at one another, mesmerized by what had taken place. The man experienced healing and freedom from the unclean spirit that had bound him and taken over his life. And the healing came on the Sabbath.

What might this have meant for the disciples who had just left everything to follow Jesus? And what are the faith lessons for us today? In the ancient Jewish tradition, the Sabbath represented a day of rest on Saturday, the seventh day of the week. The Sabbath day was set aside for reverent observance focused on the goodness, faithfulness, and mercy of God. There are some Christians today who observe the Sabbath in this way. For most Christians, however, the Sabbath is observed on Sunday, the first day of the week, commemorating the Resurrection of Jesus Christ. Taking these two traditions together, we note one is a day of rest and the other, the first day. What, then, did this mean for the man with the unclean spirit? His healing by Jesus signified the *first day* that he was free from all that he had endured under this demonic spirit. He now had the *rest* that he had longed for. This rest became his Sabbath. For the disciples, this may well have represented the first day in their lives of following Jesus and the first steps along the path of discipleship. What amazing display might take place in the spiritual realm when Jesus, by His grace, casts out the evil spirits in us as we find our way to Him and open our lives to His lordship.

CHAPTER 4

A Compelling Reflection

I sat motionless in a spirit of dismay as Jesus gazed intently out over the calm, serene, distant waters. Was He trying to process my answer to His question? Did He not believe my answer that I truly loved Him? Or did the deep waters from a distant sea out beyond the shore and the waves in some way represent my life up until this time; a life from which He had called me; what I knew well, what I had experienced, and all of the influences that had shaped me? Could it be that Jesus saw what my life's so-called fishing expedition had meant up until this time? Did He require more by way of explanation? His silent, distant stare troubled me.

I was also struck by three words He added to His question: "Do you love me *more than these?*" (John 21:15, italics mine) he asked. Could "more than these" stand for the other significant relationships in my life? Or perhaps Jesus might be thinking of the other matters in my life that I had given my loyalty and allegiance to, those earthly securities and desires that competed with my faithfulness to Him. What might my answer to His question have conjured up in His mind?

I imagine what it must have been like that day. Three years had passed since Jesus called His first four disciples to follow Him, with the promise that He would make them "fishers of men." This journey with Jesus—hearing His teachings, witnessing His miracles, seeing the compassion He had for the outcasts of society, and challenging the conventional wisdom of that culture—opened their hearts and minds to a new way of understanding the kingdom of God. Thus, Jesus's life had a profound impact on the lives of the disciples. For now, however, the life they had experienced with Jesus had apparently ended. This being the case, the disciples returned to the life they once knew—a mundane life of fishing, of casting and mending nets. Had an unproductive, weary night granted them the opportunity to consider what the past three years had meant? What had they made of recently having seen Jesus alive following His death?

A quiet, tranquil presence settled over the Sea of Galilee early that morning. The arrival of dawn slowly dispelled the darkness, casting a purple haze to the rolling hills on the distant horizon. The incoming light brought forth a warm glow of pastel pinks and oranges to the cloud formation above the hills. The only sounds were the occasional chirping and cawing of a few seagulls flying overhead and the slight lapping of the gentle waters against the side of the disciples' boat. Such beauty betrayed the hopes of the disciples disappointed after a long, mundane, unproductive night of fishing. Then came the sound of a voice shouting from the distance.

Reflecting on this event in the lives of the disciples led me to wonder if Jesus was calling me out from the life I had lived for so long, one in which I was living outside the will of God? Social drinking, partying, being captivated so much by what this world had to offer had become my lifestyle; enamored by the thrills, caught up in all the temptations of this world. Life had become something that I owed myself. The zeal I had was for my own pleasure and pursuits. Perhaps Jesus saw in me one who was not casting nets into the sea in hopes of making a great catch but one who had been throwing his life away in a meaningless quest for temporal satisfaction. Or did Jesus see one who had spent his life trying to mend and fix those matters that appeared so broken and useless?

I might add, however, that all was not lost. In my work as a law-enforcement officer and my wife's employment in the local school district as an elementary school teacher, we were fairly financially secure. God had also blessed us with two wonderful children, a son and a daughter. Aside from the many blessings God had poured out on our family, other things that came my way would be nothing more than an ephemeral vapor, nothing to grasp for a purposeful life. Little did I know at the time that, though I was "fearfully and wonderfully made" by God, as Psalm 139:14 says, I was making a mess of what He had created. Jesus's question, my response, and His momentary gaze gave rise to even more questions.

CHAPTER 5

Why Now?

Now, years after that Christmas night in 1992 when I sensed an inaudible voice saying to me, "Paul, what do you want, Me or alcohol?" I meditated on the passage from John 21 and began to understand it in a more personal and deeply spiritual sense. Jesus was not shouting out to me from a distant shore, as He did with the disciples early that morning. I wasn't in a boat, fishing and weary from a long night of having caught nothing. But I did sense a presence speaking to me, and the words carried a meaning beyond my affinity for alcohol. In essence, it was if the voice was saying to me, *"Paul, you haven't profited from the life you are living. You haven't 'caught' anything for eternal life. Come unto Me, and I will help you find what deep within your spirit you have always wanted."* I had never heard or experienced anything like this before. In looking back on that night, this sensing in my spirit was tantamount to what was spoken early that morning by the disciple, whom Jesus loved, after hearing a voice from the distant shore. "It is the Lord!" the disciple shouted (John 21:7). Like Peter upon hearing the disciple's words that night, I jumped out of my proverbial boat and made my way from the deep waters of the hopeless promises of a temporal existence to the one who could give me what I truly needed.

But why now, on this night, if I must add one more question to the many that have already been posed? What was it that enabled me to hear so clearly the choice I was being given that Christmas night of 1992? The passage of time has granted me the opportunity to reflect on God's perfect timing.

I am taken back to the night of December 27, 1992, two nights later. Shortly before our children's bedtime, our seven-year-old daughter, Lauren, came over to the couch in our living room where I had been reading. She had with her the *Beginner's Bible* we had given her and from which she had been reading to us every night. Sensing her interest in reading to me, I set aside what I had been reading and had her read to me. She was at the point where baby Moses was found floating in a basket in the river. So we read the next three short stories in the life of Moses from her Bible.

As we read, I would stop her occasionally to explain to her some point of interest or something she did not quite understand. We talked about the burning bush and how she had seen that in the movie *The Ten Commandments* and what it meant. We also talked about the different curses that God had placed on the Egyptians because their leader would not let the Israelites leave Egypt. I then explained to her the meaning of the pillar of cloud and the pillar of fire. *Oh, how I was really getting through to her!*

At some point in our conversation, Lauren asked me what the word *sacred* meant. I explained to her in the best terms I knew for her to understand how *sacred* meant something that was important to God. In explaining this, I brought up the Ark of the Covenant and told her that it was so sacred that anyone who touched it would die. This piqued her interest, and she became curious about the Ark—what it looked like and what was in it, among other things. I had mistakenly thought at that time that the first five books of the Bible written by Moses were contained in the Ark of the Covenant, so I shared this with her. I then got out a map from the back of a Bible dictionary and showed her the route of the exodus and how they carried the Ark with them. My misunderstanding of what the Ark contained in no way detracted from what Lauren was about to ask me. I could sense her little mind working much better than

15

mine when she asked, "Well, if anybody died who touched the Ark, how did they get those books out to put them in the Bible?"

Yikes! I thought. "Why do you want to ask something like that?" I asked, "Maybe it's time for you to go to bed." This happened to be the first of many times Lauren has outsmarted me over the years. Oh, my! Children have such a way of letting us adults know that we still have a lot to learn.[1]

At this particular time, I was five days away from having completed a reading of God's Word in its entirety—the task I had set out to do on January 1 of that year. I had been faithful and disciplined enough to stay with it, finding time among all the other family and work obligations and the ordinary stresses of daily life. Until that year, I was ignorant of a true understanding of the biblical narrative, having read only selected portions in order to teach a Sunday school class from time to time. Like our daughter, Lauren, perhaps I was a mere child in God's Word, weighed down with a multitude of questions, as the Bible had not been a significant part of my life. Surely the Spirit of God had tried to get my attention on other occasions, as He does for all of us. Why did I not hear it before?

One occasion, in particular, was on a night in September 1983. I, along with another agent, was assigned to work a criminal investigation in Georgetown, South Carolina. Having finished our work for the day, we ate supper at a local restaurant, after which I left for my home in Latta. As I approached the city of Conway on US Highway 501, I noticed a sign up ahead for Bob's Motel. This is the last recollection I have until I woke up on a stretcher, hearing voices as rescue squad attendants were loading me into an ambulance. I noticed blood on the front of my shirt and was immediately seized with fear. *Had I caused a wreck that injured or perhaps took the life of someone?* I had no idea at the time what had happened. Only later did I learn that a driver in another vehicle had crossed the center line of the four-lane highway and entered the westbound lane traveling east. He struck my vehicle almost head on, causing me to cross the eastbound lane, leave the highway, and land under a billboard on the other side, well off the highway. I sustained bruised ribs, a bruised kidney, and a mild concussion. How fortunate I was not to have lost my life or be severely injured.

Looking back on that incident, I cannot help but wonder if God had not been trying to get my attention then. But I just did not get it. I have no recollection of hearing anything from God then, but I realized later that only by God's grace did I survive. The truth is, I probably attributed my minor injuries to luck or coincidence. So what stood in the way of my hearing the voice of God then? Why did this critical incident not awaken me to God's presence in my life? Perhaps the answer is best explained by the mere way in which we as a culture have been conditioned to listen to the concrete voices of entertainment, television and radio talk shows, opinions in the news media, and self-help books. We are so accustomed to the "noise" of our culture and world around us that moments of sheer silence leave us anxious.

God's voice is often a mere whisper in the cacophony of a restless and busy culture. But the voice of God is witnessed in ways beyond words. Nature itself is a beautiful example of how the changing of the seasons parallel the seasons of our own lives. Yet we so often pass through them, oblivious to how our Creator is speaking to us. The simple beauty of an opened flower bud revealing perfectly ornate colors and patterns is indicative of how our hearts are opened to the resurrection hope we have in Christ Jesus. Hearts are then opened to people of all races, nations, religions, and cultures. Consider the people with whom we come into contact daily. If the Spirit of God in Christ lives in the hearts and minds of true believers—and we know that He does—why can God not speak to us through these very people, saying just the right thing at the right time to help us understand our lives at a given moment?

Years later, a passage from Paul's letter to the church in Ephesus opened my eyes to a greater understanding of just how my life was unfolding. Here Paul writes,

> You were dead through the trespasses and sins in which
> you once lived, following the course of this world,

following the ruler of the power of the air, the spirit that is now at work among those who are disobedient. All of us once lived among them in the passions of our flesh, following the desires of flesh and senses, and we were by nature children of wrath, like everyone else. But God, who is rich in mercy, out of the great love with which he loved us even when we were dead through our trespasses, made us alive together with Christ—by grace you have been saved. (Ephesians 2:1–5)

I was struck by the transitional phrase "But God" (v. 4). Yes, this was my "But God" moment when God enabled me to realize that only by His divine intervention could I have seen what my life had been and where God wanted to take me. This was a significant turning point in my life, leading me in an entirely different direction. This was my daybreak.

CHAPTER 6

Not A Settled Matter

On that Christmas night in 1992, the Lord delivered me from that which I could not let go of in my own strength. Now, in this meditation on John 21 where I envision my being with Jesus on the shore before a warm charcoal fire, I have told Him that I love Him. Now, the matter is settled. Now, hopefully, I can rest assured in His grace as if there were nothing else God had to deal with in my life. "Not so fast," in the words of one sports commentator. "Not ... so ... fast!"

In his classic work *Mere Christianity*, author C. S. Lewis writes,

> I think that many of us, when Christ has enabled us to overcome one or two sins that were an obvious nuisance, are inclined to feel (though we do not put it into words) that we are now good enough. He has done all we wanted Him to do, and we should be obliged if He would now leave us alone ... But the question is not what we intended ourselves to be, but what He intended us to be when He made us ...[2]
>
> Imagine yourself as a living house. God comes in to rebuild that house. At first, perhaps, you can understand what he is doing. He is getting the drains right and

stopping the leaks in the roof and so on: you knew that those jobs needed doing and so you are not surprised. But presently he starts knocking the house about in a way that hurts abominably and does not seem to make sense. What on earth is He up to? The explanation is that he is building quite a different house from the one you thought of—throwing out a new wing here, putting on an extra floor there, running up towers, making courtyards. You thought you were going to be made into a decent little cottage: but He is building a palace. He intends to come and live in it Himself.[3]

There are inherent dangers that sometimes lay hidden in the lives of those who surrender their lives to the lordship of Jesus Christ; vestiges or traces of our past that we tend to dismiss, neglect, or consider seemingly innocuous. An overconfident self-assurance that God has made His way into our life and cleansed us from a particular sinful attitude or behavior often leaves us blind to other areas that impede our fellowship with Him. Surely God knows what situation or circumstance one might respond to in order that her or his heart might be opened to God's saving grace. Not everyone has the same experience. I have told many people over the years that my desire for alcohol was the area of my life that God used to break into my life. Of the many life experiences I have had that led to bitter disappointment, heartache, fear, illness, or tragedy, why alcohol? Yet, the question does not end with "Why alcohol?" but "Why now?" Why did I hear this inaudible voice at this particular juncture in my life? Was I not content with God dealing only with my predilection for alcohol? Was God up to something else in my life that I just wasn't cognizant of at the time?

I must admit that I honestly believe I had experienced God's grace and deliverance in an amazing way. However, having just begun a disciplined daily reading of God's Word in January of that year, I did not associate the Ephesians passage with my experience of that Christmas night. Reflecting on it years later, I must confess that Paul's words to the church in Ephesus certainly seemed to fit my life: "You were dead through the trespasses and sins in which you once lived, following the course of this world, following the ruler of the power of the air, the spirit that is now at work among those who are disobedient" (Ephesians 2:1–2). So far, so good. Or, should I say, so far, so bad!

There was more. My attention was captured by another phrase in the Ephesians passage, a phrase that gave me a greater understanding of God's presence in my life—*even when*. I began to sense how a passage in the biblical narrative can become so real and personal for one's own life. I liken this to a geography lesson in school, where one is instructed to lay a transparency over a map in a book and see how the map has changed and the boundary lines have evolved over time. My life became the transparency placed over this passage. Without my even being consciously aware of it, I may well have been on the verge of spiritual death, like one who has had an allergic reaction to a prescribed medication and breathing has become labored until eventually he passes out. Now the clock is ticking on this person's life. An insufficient supply of oxygen to the brain can have disastrous, even fatal consequences. By some chance, someone nearby who knows CPR recognizes the person's condition and immediately begins to perform mouth-to-mouth resuscitation. Within minutes, the victim responds to the surge of oxygen he has received and slowly begins to regain consciousness. New breath has been breathed into him by a trained CPR attendant, and his life has been spared.

Could I have been at this point spiritually on Christmas night of 1992? Perhaps. So what changed? I believe God had given me the entire year of 1992 to read and study His Word. I was now attuned to God's spirit in a way that I was not in 1983 when I had the vehicle accident. Although I was reading through the Bible for the first time, spiritually I was like an infant at its mother's breast—getting nourished just enough to be sensitive to something significant taking place. God broke through to me in the reading of His Word—*even when* I was dead through my trespasses. In the words of that traditional hymn of the faith, "Breathe on Me Breath of God, fill me with life anew,"[4] immersing myself in God's Holy Word was like learning to breathe all over again. What could have been spiritual death for me was now life restored, and now I could breathe in Christ. Coming to the realization of what my life had been, I now had a new perspective on life. The Spirit of God opened my eyes on that Christmas night and breathed new life into me. Only He could have done for me what I could not do for myself. Years later, God allowed me to be a part of another story of deliverance, a way that I desperately needed to learn as a faith lesson for further spiritual growth.

CHAPTER 7

All Is Well

"Do you love me?" So how do we answer this question that genuinely demonstrates Jesus Christ as Lord of our lives? God puts before us in specific seasons of our lives people through whom we can offer a tangible response of our love for Christ.

One appointed time and location came for me on Saturday, November 23, 2013. I had rented a vendor space at the Wellness Center in Dillon, South Carolina, for the annual Fall Holiday Festival, in hopes of selling copies of a Christian devotional book I had written. I had made all of the necessary preparations, with a sign for each end of the book table, along with bookmarks and postcards giving interested readers a description of the book. As a first-time author, I had no experience in promoting my work; nor did I know what to expect in a venue of this type. For someone who finds selling tickets for barbeque take-out plates for a fundraiser a drudgery, selling a book is quite a venture. During the day, some would walk by looking on, while a few would pick up the book, flip through it, lay it down, and move to the next booth or table. And yes, I did manage to sell seventeen copies that day. Oh, what a way to make a living! I found the publishing process fascinating and learned that to write to impress others, to become wealthy, or to gain popularity is writing for all the wrong reasons, although this was not my purpose. Mine was a personal endeavor to enable others to understand how God puts people in our paths from time to time to shape us spiritually. Little did I know that fall afternoon what God had set in motion in my life.

Early that afternoon, a lady by the name of Pearl Nettles came by my table. I knew Pearl from the small town in which we lived and also through the school we attended. But most importantly, Pearl was my mother and father's nurse at Marion County Medical Center during the waning days of their lives. She attended to both of them with the greatest of care. Pearl spoke with me and said she wanted one of my books for her brother, Willie. The mention of Willie's name called to my mind the individual who had attended to Sandra and Clay Roberts following the wreck on Highway 917 outside of Latta the year earlier. I did not know Willie personally but had heard his name mentioned over the years. She spoke with me about some of the issues Willie had dealt with and some of the struggles he had endured in recent years. Pearl purchased a book and before leaving said, "Paul, if you have time later on, will you go over to the booth where Willie is and talk with him?" She pointed in the direction of Willie's spot at the festival, where he was selling some of his wood crafts.

Later, as the crowd thinned out and the sales did not look promising, I left my table and walked over to where Pearl had pointed. I passed by a couple of vendor spaces before coming to a space with a tall divider from which hung many wooden plaques and artifacts. Seated in a chair in front of the display, Willie recognized me and welcomed me. I sat down, and we talked for several minutes as he showed me some of his woodwork. He asked me to come out to his house sometime. I agreed that I would like to do this and then returned to my table.

Months passed, and neither Willie nor I saw or heard from one another. Then one day, I received a call from Willie. He spoke for a few minutes, reminding me of our conversation at the Holiday Festival and how we spoke of getting together one day soon. He asked me to come out to see him sometime. I said, "Well, I can come now if that's okay." He said that would be just fine. So I drove to his home several miles away, and upon arriving, entered a garage-type area where Willie did his refinishing work. For about an hour and a half that day, we talked, giving me the opportunity to learn more about Willie. His openness and his willingness to share some of his personal struggles left me feeling as if I was his closest confidant. Willie shared openly with me about his past with drugs and alcohol and the problems these had created in his life and in his relationships with others. By his own admission, Willie led a somewhat rowdy and rambunctious (my words) life in the past. As my mother used to say, "He made no bones about it." On this particular day, Willie told me that a couple of years earlier, he found himself in dire straits, incarcerated in the Dillon County Jail, in a situation from which he desperately needed deliverance. He got down on his knees and cried out to the Lord that if God would rescue him from his plight, he would never drink again and would serve God for the rest of his life. No sooner had he ended his prayer than Sandy, his sister, and a friend of Willie's came in to take him home.

This was a turning point in Willie's life. The light of Christ had dawned in Willie's life, granting him an overwhelming sense of God's presence. God had answered Willie's prayer, and Willie kept his vow. Sensing how God had set him free from alcohol, Willie felt a deep desire to get to know as much about God as he could. He immersed himself in the daily reading of scripture. His increasing knowledge of God's Word brought him into a deeper relationship with the Lord and gave him the strength to refrain from substance abuse in any form. Willie let it go because he found something, or should I say someone, far better than the life he had been living. And he never drank again after that day. He later became very active in Alcoholics Anonymous, sponsoring others and later led some of the group sessions. In the time I had with Willie that day, I sensed that this may well be someone I would connect with in a deeper, more personal way. The time we had was meaningful and the conversation fruitful. Etched in my memory is a request that Willie made of me toward the end of our time together. Willie was not driving at the time, having lost his license due to an automobile accident, so he asked if I could come out there on the upcoming Sunday and take him to the Sunday school class I attended. He said, "Paul, I want to surprise Michael Bethea." He shared with me that he and Michael were longtime friends, best friends in high school, and they had continued to remain in close contact over the years. It was Michael whom Willie could lean on in difficult times and with whom Willie could pour out his heart. They shared a kindred spirit.

I did as he asked, picking Willie up at his home the following Sunday morning and driving him to the United Methodist Church in Latta. As Willie entered the men's Sunday school hut, Michael caught a glimpse of him and was flabbergasted. He grinned, they greeted one another, spoke briefly, and Willie took a seat. It was on this day that Willie became very much a part of Latta UMC, becoming reacquainted with many friends from his past. I recall watching as some would come up to him at the end of the worship service and give him the warmest hug, overjoyed to see him.

Over the ensuing two and a half years from the time I first met Willie at his home, our relationship grew in a deeply meaningful way, both personally and spiritually. We developed a spiritual bond. We would talk regularly on the telephone. Whenever I called him, he would answer by saying, "Hello, Paul Gasque," with a hint of enthusiasm in his voice. We would text back and forth, almost daily, as he would with so many others, and often with his referencing a particular passage of scripture that touched him spiritually. Regardless of what he might have been wrestling with at that time, that which concerned him deeply, he could say with confidence at the conclusion of the phone call or the text, "All's well, Paul. All is well."

In the following months, Laura witnessed the relationship that Willie and I had and in her discerning spirit reminded me that my ultimate purpose in being at the Wellness Center in Dillon that fall day in 2013 was not to sell books but to meet Willie Nettles.

I learned early on in my relationship with Willie that he possessed a valuable gift. His paternal grandfather, whom the grandchildren knew affectionately as "Big Daddy," worked as a furniture upholsterer in the nearby town of Marion, South Carolina. Willie's father worked with "Big Daddy," refinishing the wooden legs and the armrests of the furniture. As the years passed, Willie's dad became more adept at refinishing bigger pieces of furniture and taught this skill to Willie and his sisters at an early age. At the time I met Willie, this had become his livelihood. Often he would show me a piece of furniture that he had restored or was in the process of restoring. He had a knack for making the worst, most dilapidated item of furniture look brand new. What I soon saw, however, revealed something even more profound—the hand of God working in Willie's life and manifested in his woodwork. He once had me look at a piece he was working on, pointing out a place that needed some additional work. I said, "You know, Willie, there's a spiritual message in what you are doing here. This is much like how God works in our lives. We see ourselves and one another as we are. God sees us as we will be."

"Ah! Yes, Paul, you are so right," Willie said, as if he had already realized this. I can only imagine what must have occupied Willie's mind as he stripped off the old, rough and scratched finish of a piece of furniture, smoothed out and restored the rough edges before applying the final coats. Then, after all the time he had put into this piece, stepping back and looking with admiration on what it had now become. I am inclined to think that deep within Willie's subconscious, there was a sense of God's presence doing a similar work in him. Without his being aware of it at the time, Willie's gift for woodwork ministered back to me in many ways by what the Lord revealed to me through him. As we open our hearts and minds to God, He takes the broken and the damaged parts of our lives and puts them back together again, restoring us over the course of our lives to what He has created us to be.

An emotional moment for me in my relationship with Willie came a couple of weeks before Christmas 2015. In our conversations, I sensed that Willie was struggling financially. He never asked for money or anything materially but needed more work at the time to satisfy some of his financial obligations. We all know the burden and hardship this imposes on every facet of one's life. My sensing

Willie's concern became like a little seed planted in me that began to slowly germinate in my mind and heart. I took it upon myself, without Willie's knowledge or consent, to contact some of his friends who had known him over the years and had been in contact with him through the church. I shared discreetly with them Willie's concern, assuring them that Willie had not asked for this, nor did he know that I would be bringing this to their attention. In just a few days, we had collected $700 to assist Willie with his financial needs.

The following Saturday morning, I called Michael Bethea and asked if he would like to go with me to take the money to Willie. He agreed, and we called Willie and asked if we could meet with him for a few minutes. Willie gladly welcomed us out to his house. Upon our arrival, Willie greeted us at the side entrance that led into the converted garage serving as a shop for his woodworking business. He ushered us up the stairs leading to the kitchen and den of his home. Michael and I took a seat on a small couch facing the fireplace located across the room, and Willie sat down in a chair next to the fireplace. After a few casual greetings, we told Willie that we had something for him. We handed him an envelope containing a Christmas greeting card. Willie took it and looked over at us, hesitating briefly before opening the envelope. He tapped the envelope on his leg as he continued to talk. Looking over at us, Willie then unsealed the envelope and removed the card. He read the Christmas greeting and then opened the card. As he did, he saw the cash inside. He paused and grew silent for a moment, as if in a state of disbelief. Overwhelmed by what he found, he said, "Paul, Michael, y'all didn't have to do this. I cannot believe y'all did this."

"Willie, you have a lot of people who care a lot about you," I told him. "No, we didn't have to do this, and it didn't take much of an effort. Once we made a few phone calls and more people heard about it, they joined in. We didn't put your business in the street, Willie. Just told them that you were going through a hard time right now."

Willie leaned over in his chair, put both hands over his face,

28

and began to weep. He remained silent for a couple of minutes as his way of trying to take it all in. I looked over at Michael, seated to my left, and noticed tears welling up in his eyes. Gaining his composure moments later, Willie leaned back in his chair with teary eyes and through a voice breaking with emotion said, "You have no idea what this means. This is the first Christmas that I can remember when I did not have any money to buy gifts for people, and now this. I can't believe it." Trying to meet his monthly financial obligations had stretched Willie to the limit. He lavished his gratitude for those who contributed to this, though we never told him who the donors were. Our conversation turned briefly to other matters going on in our lives. Soon afterward, Michael and I got ready to leave, but not before Willie, a South Carolina Gamecock fan, had to give Michael a little ribbing about Michael's Clemson Tigers. Willie managed one of his mischievous grins as he waited for Michael's reaction. We all had a good laugh, and Michael and I got into the car and left for home.

The true meaning of what this outreach to Willie represented eluded me at that time. Only later, and even up until the writing of this book, did I capture the true essence of what it meant to him. It wasn't so much the money that seized him emotionally, even though the need was great, but the friends and relationships that such a gift represented. "Y'all," he said, as he responded to this generous offering that day, a common expression especially in the South as a reference to a group we are in the company of or are speaking to. But here, the meaning took on an even greater significance. "Y'all" indicated some of the people in Willie's life, those cherished friends who had stuck with him over the years and who likewise valued his friendship. Only later did I learn that Willie texted scripture verses almost daily to a plethora of his friends, often relating how a particular passage of scripture spoke to him in his faith journey. I had even come to expect an inspirational text message from Willie most mornings, some sent even before I had awakened, indicating the kindred spirit we shared that began at the fall festival in Dillon in November 2013.

As much as Willie's community of friends and fellow believers meant to him, his time of quiet solitude in God's Word and his daily devotional readings and reflections bore equal importance. He was an avid reader, especially of American history and Christian literature. He knew the importance of seeking the Lord and growing in his relationship with Jesus Christ; his time alone on those early mornings served him well in seeking the heart of God. He loved the Christian classics. In the two and a half years that I knew him, Willie read *Mere Christianity* by C. S. Lewis, *The Practice of the Presence of God* by Brother Lawrence, and had a copy of *The Cost of Discipleship* by Dietrich Bonhoeffer. His interest in these books called to my mind the parable of Jesus from the gospel of Mark. In the parable, someone had scattered seed on the ground. In the days that followed, the seed sprouted and began to grow. Willie's devotional time and his interest in these readings were evidence that the seed of Jesus Christ planted earlier in Willie's heart and mind was growing. This sacred time in Willie's life bore precious fruit in our relationship, as we often shared our personal insights in our time together. Willie's appetite for God's Word led to his willingness to teach on occasions at the men's Sunday school at Latta United Methodist Church.

CHAPTER 8

All That Matters

"Dec. 7, 2016, 10:33 AM," the heading read. Another text from Willie.

2nd Cor., 5:16–21, 6:1–2

> These are Wonderful. To be reconciled and to be able to be reconciled with Him forever.
>
> He heard me and He stepped in Paul. My life will never be without now. I am so Thankful. Things that seemed so important, just are not anymore. To be in a relationship with Christ, is all that matters. He is with us.
>
> To know He is with me and us, is the most comforting thing we carry.[5]

Over the ensuing year leading up to this day, Willie and I had spent a considerable amount of time together. I came to know Willie even better as he shared with me some of his life experiences in his family, his high school years, and the time he spent at Western Wyoming Community College, where he obtained an associate of applied science degree in natural gas compression technology. Willie also spoke candidly about his involvement with drugs and alcohol and the hardships this lifestyle had created for him. He had lost his driving privileges as the result of an automobile accident but anxiously awaited the restoration of that privilege in March 2017. This would give him a renewed sense of freedom and would enhance his woodworking business in getting items of furniture transported to and from customers' homes and businesses. For the time being, when the need arose, some of his friends, including me, would drive Willie to various locations.

I often think about the biweekly trips he and I made, whenever I happen to pass the intersection at the Highway 501 bypass where Willie and I would cross over on our way to nearby Florence. These trips allowed us to talk freely about family issues, college football, and yes, politics. The presidential election was drawing closer, and Willie seemed captivated by it. I had to remain cautious, as we did not always agree about certain issues. There were even times when Willie would mention some issue that he thought I differed with him about, and he would look over at me with that sly grin of his, waiting to hear what I had to say. "Is that right?" would sometimes be my comment (usually a safe response), and I drove on.

Willie, in turn, would say, "Yes, Paul, *you* know," with that slow, deliberate drawl of his. This never became an issue in our relationship, but it did make for interesting conversation nonetheless.

Our trips to Florence gave rise to some of the more meaningful conversations that Willie and I shared. Out of frustration, sometimes anger and even despair, Willie poured out his heart over some of the personal concerns that weighed heavily upon him. There were times when matters seemed hopeful and encouraging and other times when any progress that had been made fell apart. As so often

32

is the case, even in our own lives, neither he nor I had the answers to what troubled Willie, but his being able to empty himself of it all brought him some consolation. Willie found strength and support in the men's Sunday school class, even teaching the lesson at times. He also found a church family with the congregation of Latta United Methodist Church that allowed him to reconnect with many of his friends from the past.

One day on our way to Florence, Willie said, "You know, Paul, I really want to get up in church and share with the people what the church has meant to me. I just can't bring myself to do it right now."

I said, "Willie, there will be time for you to do that, and you will know when it is right." He brought this up again a couple of weeks later.

Also, during this time, Willie led regular group sessions of Alcoholics Anonymous and had sponsored others to join the group. Relationships were very much a part of Willie's life and his spiritual healing. He had come to realize and experience the importance of bearing one another's burdens. I recall him telling me on more than one occasion, "Paul, if I ever start drinking again, I will be much worse than I was before, much worse." But Willie remained steadfast.

Looking back on the words from his December 7 text that Willie found so wonderful compels me to share this passage with you. Here the apostle Paul writes to the church in Corinth:

> From now on, therefore, we regard no one from a human point of view; even though we once knew Christ from a human point of view, we know him no longer in that way. So if anyone is in Christ, there is a new creation: everything old has passed away; see, everything has become new! All this is from God, who reconciled us to himself through Christ, and has given us the ministry of reconciliation; that is, in Christ God was reconciling the world to himself, not counting their trespasses against them, and entrusting the message of reconciliation to us. So we are ambassadors for Christ, since God is

making his appeal through us; we entreat you on behalf of Christ, be reconciled to God. For our sake he made him to be sin who knew no sin, so that in him we might become the righteousness of God.

As we work together with him, we urge you also not to accept the grace of God in vain. For he says,

"At an acceptable time I have listened to you, and on a day of salvation I have helped you."

See, now is the acceptable time; see, now is the day of salvation!

(2 Corinthians 5:16–6:2)

Today, in this age of communication and computer technology, handwritten notes and letters are slowly becoming a thing of the past, a lost art, superseded in part by the convenience and swiftness of text messaging. Yet, even for those of us who are frequent texters, many of us treasure personal handwritten notes or letters because they can be read over and over again, usually in search of some meaning beyond what the words themselves express. Mere words, however eloquent, do not always fully express what the writer wants to convey. With this in mind, I delved into these words from the scripture passage sent to me by Willie in search of a deeper understanding of how these words ministered to him.

I thought back on the day when Willie found himself incarcerated in the Dillon County Jail and the promise he made to God that if God would release him from there, Willie would never drink again. I assumed this held true for drug involvement also. The answer came for Willie when his sister and a friend showed up almost immediately to have him released. This marked the beginning of a journey for Willie; not just a matter of giving something up but leading him to something even greater for his own life. He had personally experienced God's grace.

The text sent to me by Willie on the morning of December 7 caused me to believe that this was Willie's quest, to attain for himself by God's grace what God had ultimately wanted for him. In the words of the prophet Isaiah, "For thus said the Lord GOD, the Holy One of Israel: In returning and rest you shall be saved;

in quietness and in trust shall be your strength" (Isaiah 30:15). Had Willie found it that day? Perhaps so. The apostle Paul opens the segment of his letter to the Corinthian church sent to me by Willie with the words "From now on" (2 Corinthians 5:16). Willie mentions in his text, "My life will never be without *now*" (italics are mine). Willie had the assurance of being forgiven of his sins and being reconciled unto God in Christ Jesus. *"See, now is the acceptable time; see, now is the day of salvation!"* (2 Corinthians 6:2b). Paul writes.

CHAPTER 9

Heartbreak

The telephone rang in our home on the morning of Monday, December 12, 2016. I had retreated earlier to the bedroom once occupied by our son, Conan, who no longer lived with us. Laura settled in the kitchen for her quiet devotional time. We find it necessary at times to honor the solitude and privacy of one another's sacramental moments of Bible reading and reflection. I managed to hear her answer the telephone, followed by a few moments of silence. Then I heard her scream, "What! No! No!" She continued talking to the caller and then rushed into the bedroom where I was. I had not heard from Willie since the text I received on Wednesday. Laura handed me the phone with a look of anguish and tears in her eyes.

"Paul, Willie's house burned to the ground last night, and Willie didn't make it out. Willie's dead, Paul," Laura cried out.

I immediately grabbed the phone. It was Willie's sister, Pearl. She shared the news with me. I could not believe it, nor did I want to believe it. By this time, I had walked into the kitchen, still talking on the phone. Pearl related to me all she knew at that time. Once my conversation with Pearl ended, I clicked the end button, laid the phone down, put my head down on the table, and cried and cried. The pain of having lost a dear friend, and in such a tragic way, was more than I could handle. Two and a half years had passed since I first became acquainted with Willie. But in that time, we had developed a deep, personal relationship grounded in our faith in Jesus Christ. I can safely say that I had never had a spiritual relationship with another man like I had with Willie. We were bonded together in Christ Jesus. A friendship we both needed.

The following days left me wondering what had happened. I thought back on the text Willie sent to me the previous Wednesday. What might have been Willie's activities the past four days? Had anyone else heard from him? If so, who? And the fire? What caused it, and what was Willie's condition at the time? This myriad of questions haunted me. A significant aspect of my life over the past two and a half years, which had meant so much to me, had ended and so abruptly.

A day or so later, the family called to ask if I would preside at Willie's funeral. I had anticipated that they might request this and was honored that they did, but it would be a difficult task, taxing my emotions to the limit. *How would I be able to maintain my composure?* God would give me the strength, I knew. Honoring Willie's memory would be the last thing I could do for him, and yet I had known him personally for only a brief span of his life. There were many others who knew him longer and better than I, but our relationship was that of walking a spiritual path together. I obliged by offering to lead the funeral service, which was scheduled for Saturday, December 17, at Latta United Methodist Church.

At the appointed hour that Saturday, the service was set to begin. The friends and family had gathered and taken their seats in the sanctuary. During the service, a personal friend of Willie's offered a moving testimony of the impact Willie had had on his life. I would follow with the eulogy. What I witnessed during the service truly amazed me. In my thirteen years of pastoral ministry and in other funeral services I had attended over the years, I do not recall a more diverse group of people than what I saw at Willie's funeral that day. Certainly, a testimony to the kind of people who were, in some measure, a part of Willie's life. Yes, I believe there are those occasions when what constitutes the crowd bears a stronger witness than its mere size. When the time came for me to offer the eulogy, I opened with these words:

The occasion for which we are here today is, without question, the last thing I thought I would be doing this Saturday afternoon. But it is the one for which I feel most honored—to honor the memory of my friend Willie Nettles. In this festive season of the year, we often find ourselves caught up in trying to find the right gift for those special people in our lives. And yet, the most cherished gift does not always come wrapped in a box or a package with a decorative bow. God has a way of blessing us beyond all that we could ever ask or imagine. The greatest gift of all came to us on that silent and holy night two thousand years ago in a remote little village called Bethlehem. It is not a story that ended in that quiet place long, long ago. It is one that continues to be told and lived out in our own lives today as Christ continues to come to us through people we encounter on life's journey. One of those people who I can easily call a gift from God was Willie Nettles, whom God put into my life in the fall of 2013.

Three days ago, I could not have done what I hope to be able to do today in eulogizing Willie. My relationship with him was one of the most uplifting and meaningful relationships I have ever had, although I knew him for only about three years. And when we lose someone so dear to us, we have to ask ourselves what we learned from our friend that serves to make us better persons.[6]

There were moments during the eulogy when I fought back my emotions, evident through my broken voice. But I managed to get through it. At the conclusion of the service in the church, the congregants were invited and directed to the Floyd Dale landing of the Little Pee Dee River several miles away. Here the service would conclude with personal remembrances from Willie's friends, after which Willie's ashes would be scattered in the river, as was done a few years earlier for Lil, Willie's sister. I looked on that day with a deep sense of loss as Willie's sisters, Pearl and Sandy, made their way to the edge of the landing and scattered Willie's ashes into the gently flowing waters of the Little Pee Dee River. The crowd watched in silent reverence as what remained of our dear friend slowly drifted away, coincidentally on the same date as his deceased sister's birthday. Minutes later, as Laura and I left the landing to return to our car, we could see tears and the emotional pain on the faces of those present. What did not leave me that day but has remained with me has been the memories of those two and a half years that I had to get to know Willie. I have no doubt that this was God's grace in my life. Looking back on that season in my life has enabled me to understand that God in Christ Jesus had a faith lesson to teach me through my relationship with Willie. Something deep within my spirit needed to be fed, which I will share in the last section of this book.

CHAPTER 10

Looking Back

I assure Jesus that I do love Him. He turns His gaze from the distant waters and looks toward me. He then directs His attention to the crackling fire and to coals that had settled into a glowing heap. He gently stirs the fire with a small tree branch He holds in His hand as sparks rise from the ashes. Then He says, "Feed my lambs" (John 21:15b). *My* lambs, He emphasizes.

Hmm, I think. *I have just told Him that I love Him. Why is this necessary? What might feeding His "lambs" have to do with my loving Him?* My thoughts then turn to how He once described Himself. He called Himself the shepherd and how the sheep hear His voice as He calls them by name and leads them out to green pastures and still waters. And the sheep follow Him and are sustained by His guidance. I was suddenly struck by a thought from my own life as I pondered those words. I was once one of those lambs, so to speak, dependent upon the upbringing, the nourishment and support of loving parents. Like a lamb, I was totally dependent upon other people. The upbringing in our home, the spiritual nurture from a church family as a young child, Sunday school teachers, nighttime Bible stories read to me by my mom and the many other life-nurturing experiences were all ways that I, the lamb, was being fed. I was continually guided, protected, provided for, and watched over by others.

It was in my childhood years that I was stricken with a severe case of the measles, which resulted in a high fever. Not long after recovering from the measles, my parents noticed something peculiar about me, unlike anything they had seen before. Occasionally, my eyes would roll back in my head, my eyelids would flutter, and I would temporarily lose all awareness of my surroundings, eventually urinating on myself. My parents felt for a while that I was doing this for attention, only the urination part made no sense to them. Noticing that the seizures were not stopping, they decided to take me to a doctor to seek some explanation or diagnosis. It was later determined that I suffered from petit mal epilepsy. Not much was known about epilepsy in our locale at that time, certainly not by my parents. I recall their taking me to several doctors in order to have me examined and to determine the best treatment regimen for me. This often involved several adjustments in my medication. One physician I especially recall was a Filipino woman at Johns Hopkins Medical Center in Baltimore, Maryland. I had never seen a woman doctor before, especially a foreign one. But she was wonderful and seemed to have an adept understanding of what I was going through. I only wish I could remember her name.

My most vivid recollections of those years were the humiliation I experienced when I would urinate in my pants in class during elementary school and try to hide it during the day. There was another time, one summer, when we were at our family cottage at Windy Hill Beach, South Carolina. Our neighbors from the beach house next door happened to be there that same week and were visiting in our home at the time. While several of us were together in the front family room, I was stricken by a seizure. Mama managed to get me to a bedroom in the back of the house, away from the others, and sat there with me until the seizure abated and I calmed down. Coming to my senses, I cried from the embarrassment of others seeing me in this way and of having to be taken to another room. I felt so different at the time. The seizures were eventually controlled by the proper medication, and

I grew out of the epilepsy around the age of twelve or thirteen. It is believed that my condition might have been caused by the high fever I sustained during my bout with the measles.

My youth and adolescent years were also complicated by two other health concerns. I developed a serious case of asthma and more than a dozen different allergies. Laboring to breathe and sneezing repeatedly made life difficult at times. Breathing treatments and allergy shots were not something I relished the thought of, but I did get accustomed to them eventually.

I could share much more about my health issues during my youth, but I have no medical records at my disposal to serve my recollection. What I have shared comes directly from memory. The point of it all is that, yes, Mary Elizabeth Gasque (my mom) had a little lamb, one that needed careful and attentive nurturing. Writing this book and reviewing the entry in my spiritual journal on the passage from John chapter 21 has allowed me to reflect on those difficult years of my life and to recognize who I was as a helpless lamb in need of constant, attentive, loving care. Christ made all this possible for me to receive. This, in turn, allows the words of Jesus to "feed His lambs" to resonate deeply within me for His eternal purposes.

CHAPTER 11

Tending the Sheep

A cool, gentle breeze coming in off the open sea brushes lightly against us as we sit in momentary silence. Jesus now looks into the flames of the fire dancing from the wind and watches as the smoke sweeps overhead in the direction of the tree line off to His right. Hopefully, I have pleased Him and assured Him with my answer that I love Him. Once again, the silence is broken as He looks over at me more intently now and asks, "Paul, do you love Me?" *Why might He be asking this of me again? What is He trying to find out from me? He does know, does He not, that I truly love Him? But He has a reason for asking.* I pause slightly and watch as He picks up the stick that He had laid down by His side earlier and again begins to stoke the fire. I am wrestling with the thought of where this conversation is headed. The flames are awakened even more and begin to burn brighter, stealing away the remaining darkness of the dawn that surrounds us. Jesus is ruminating over the fire that is burning brighter now, as if to await my answer.

"Please know, my Lord, that I love you," I respond.

With His eyes still gazing into the fire, Jesus says to me, "Tend My sheep." A minute or so passes, and we are engulfed in a silence that blots out any of the surrounding noises that would ordinarily capture our attention. By now, I am wondering what all this could mean.

"Tend my sheep" (John 21:16b). The very thought of tending sheep conjures up in my mind those years when I progressed both physically and mentally from my childhood to my adolescence and teenage years. A certain level of maturity developed in me (or so I thought!) as I moved from dependence upon others to a greater independence of my own. (What a nice way of saying there were times when no one could tell me anything!) My thinking and actions gradually evolved into and were somewhat influenced by the world around me. By the mid-1960s, I had become enamored by the Beatles, as were so many others. What great strides were being made technologically! I recall my older brother coming home very excited one day from the country diner across the street from where we lived. *What was the big deal?* I thought. He shared that he had just watched *Gomer Pyle* in color. We had never seen a color television before that time.

Beyond the small-town world that we were accustomed to, a controversial war raged on in Vietnam, with angry protests cropping up in Washington, DC, and around the country. Racial tensions escalated in the South. Peaceful marches demanding civil rights sometimes resulted in eruptions of violence. The assassinations of Martin Luther King Jr. in April 1968 and Robert Kennedy in June of that same year sent shockwaves around an already disquieted nation. I recall my mother waking me one morning to tell me that Robert Kennedy had been killed the night before. As a fifteen-year-old, I was not attuned to much of the nation's political climate at that time. The hippie culture with its plethora of psychedelic drugs was in full force. Woodstock and the Manson Gang murders came the following year in 1969. Many young people seemed to be trying to find themselves in such a disordered culture. Making mature and responsible choices in such times was difficult for young teenagers. My senior year in high school, 1971, would later become the first year for full racial integration at Latta High School.

From a personal standpoint, much of what concerned me was what others thought of me, how I appeared to those around me, how well I performed in athletics and academics, who my friends were, and so on. Such a mindset can be beneficial and motivating but also detrimental. Many of the decisions I made were obviously not well thought out and certainly not to my well-being. Yes, I can honestly admit that this represented the "sheep" stage of my life, as I was one for whom careful attending was needed. Reflecting on that time, I can see how I had strayed from the flock at times. Yet, my life experience over the years has taught me that there never comes a time in one's life when some measure of attending is not needed, perhaps in encouragement, in accountability, in bearing another's burden, or in caring for an elderly parent or loved one. We all find ourselves tending to those we genuinely care for. The nurturing and the care we have received throughout our lives have schooled us in how to help others in difficult times. I am forever grateful to my parents, grandparents, pastors, teachers in both school and Sunday school, athletic coaches, friends, and others who assumed some role in shaping me and guiding me along life's path with their patience and their attentive understanding.

My answering the call into pastoral ministry many years later granted me an even greater understanding of the importance of tending Christ's sheep. Attentive care and visitation of parishioners is a vital aspect of a pastor's ministry, especially for older parishioners. Funerals, in addition to hospital, nursing home, and even residential visits, consume much of the pastor's time. Several years ago, I visited with an elderly lady from one of the churches I pastored at that time. Iva Lee had been active in the life of the church for many years, but the progressive onset of dementia had rendered her virtually homebound. What I remember most about her from her active years was that she loved to cook, especially desserts. At church functions where a meal was provided, she would occasionally slip me a few of her tantalizing seven-layer cookies to take home. I always looked forward to the church luncheons and other festivities at the church because of some of the goodies provided by the ladies. In fact, in 2006 while appointed to Trinity and Berea United Methodist churches in Marlboro County, I was diagnosed with type-2 diabetes. I often joked with some of the members that the churches must have contributed to my diabetes. Certainly, the church food had nothing to do with this, but it helps to put the blame on something other than oneself, right?

It was at a nursing home in Florence, South Carolina, that I had occasion to visit with Iva Lee, where she was a resident. I was directed to her room and, upon entering, greeted her joyfully, telling her how good it was to see her. I sat down on one side of her bed, and she was in a wheelchair a few feet away. She seemed to recognize who I was, and after visiting with her for a few minutes of exchanged greetings, I noticed her fumbling with the buttons on her blouse. We continued to talk, and she continued to work with the buttons. I did not really pay that much attention to what she was doing until I saw her blouse begin to open. To my surprise, she had unbuttoned her blouse completely. I was shocked! I thought to myself, *I've got to get a nurse or someone to rescue me from this.* So I darted immediately out of the room to the nearest nurses' station. I didn't wait for anyone to ask if they could help me. I took the initiative and said, "Ma'am, uh, I need some help in Mrs. Iva Lee's room. She has unbuttoned and opened her blouse, and I need you to get it back like it was." The nurse, (I'll call her the attendant now, because I was in desperate need of being attended to myself by this time), walked quickly to the room. Finding her blouse open, the attendant said, "Why, Mrs. Iva Lee, what are you doing? You can't take off your blouse with the preacher here. Let's button it back now."

Mrs. Iva Lee said without hesitation, "Well, the preacher asked me to do it."

Help! Lord, save me! This was not the kind of tending to I had in mind with Mrs. Iva Lee that day. In fact, after this, I became the one in need of careful attending to.

So what might these words of Jesus mean to me in the world in which I live? What might a life of "tending the sheep" of Christ look like in such an individualistic, greedy, self-serving, and hostile world? Sheep, by nature, are utterly helpless animals, continuously dependent on their shepherd to guide them to lush, green, open pastures to graze; to lead them to calm, still waters that pose no threat from a fast-moving current. They easily go astray, requiring the shepherd to leave the flock to bring them back. When injured, sheep need the careful attention of the shepherd to treat their wounds and monitor their healing. And sheep are always in need of protection from predators.

I go back to the opening line of Psalm 23: "The Lord is my shepherd" (v. 1). The very words of this verse connote a contentment rooted in relationship. Knowing who Christ is and has been for me forms the basis for that which He has called me. In essence, what we find most satisfying, needful, and meaningful for life is not what we have or what we can acquire. It is found in relationship—a relationship with Jesus Christ as Lord of our lives, the Shepherd who makes possible all we need for our daily lives. As our Shepherd, Jesus goes before us in the faith, preparing the way ahead and leading us to places where we may never have been before (paraphrase of Joshua 3:3–4). He has charted our course in life and has given us the assurance that He will provide for our earthly needs along the way. This assurance instills in us the confidence that we are never alone and our willingness to rest in His all-sufficient grace and love. A culture that does not know Christ in this way, that does not give Christ the sovereign rule and reign over its life, can never be content with not wanting more. Materialism has become its idol. The more we have, the more we place our security on our possessions and wealth, the further we stray from the Lord and from one another. Seeking personal satisfaction in an effort to impress others with our wealth blinds us to the heavenly treasures that await us as God's children. "Take delight in the LORD," the psalmist writes, "and he will give you the desires of your heart" (Psalm 37:4).

Laura and I served in pastoral ministry for nine and thirteen years respectively. Since our retirements and Laura's subsequent retirement from the public school system, we have found ourselves financially unable to support some of the charitable organizations we used to support. This reduction in our financial status, however, eventually led to unexpected results. Over time, I began to find myself in the company of people whose lives were not identified with luxury and affluence. Some were living in dire circumstances. Some struggled with health-related issues; for others, it was financial, social, and family related, and for one, the issue was homelessness. Among the various issues were people I did not know or was not closely associated with, but I found them to be truly loving and wonderful people. In reflecting on these people and situations, I am led to believe that what was once my ability to give in terms of money has now taken on a new role. I am convinced that God is now calling me to give my time, which has become more available to me. This conjures up the image in my mind of how Jesus Christ, the Great Shepherd, has directed my path into the company of people whom He is calling me to come alongside spiritually as a helper and encourager. Most importantly, I have found that it is through these people that Jesus seeks to reveal Himself to me.

One such opportunity for Laura came just prior to the writing of this book. After being retired for five years, Laura was given an opportunity to teach a homebound student. She had maintained her teacher's certification but was not knowledgeable about or had any experience in working with someone with an incapacitating medical condition. Laura would be working with others in the local elementary school system, people whom she had worked with in previous years. One of the other teachers remarked that this was a "divine appointment" for Laura, suggesting that God, not the school district, had called Laura to this task. How unfortunate it is that we Christians fail to recognize the true meaning of such situations, dismissing them as good favors returned, when in fact they may well be "divine appointments," God at work in not-so-obvious ways. The needs we have in our own lives and the need we as Christians can fulfill in the lives of others is one of the ways in which we can say, "Yes, Lord, You know that I love You."

CHAPTER 12

I Thought I Knew Who I Was

Umm! he thought. *That's strange. I haven't noticed this before.*
The month of March in northeastern South Carolina often ushers in sporadic weather changes. The transition of winter into spring often comes with some resistance from Mother Nature. Warm, sunny days call out the seasonal wardrobe and outdoor grilling fever, only to be tempered within a couple of days by chilly, even cold and windy afternoons with occasional heavy rain showers. On one particular cool morning in March 2014, David Watson, a local attorney and a close friend of mine, ventured out of his home in the Temperance Hill community of Marion County. As he was making his way across the lawn, the sprinkler from an underground irrigation system came on. Unable to avoid the spray, the entire front of David's shirt got wet. David was struck, however, by the realization that he had no sensation from the cold water that had dampened the right side of his shirt and chest but could clearly be felt on the left side. He suspected that he had a physical concern that needed immediate medical attention.

David and I have known one another all our lives. I consider him a dear friend and a close personal confidant. We attended school in Latta from our elementary years until high school graduation. We were among the seventeen Latta High School graduates of 1971 who were members of the Latta United Methodist Church. Following high school and college, David later enrolled in law school at the University of Alabama in Birmingham, transferring the following year to the University of South Carolina Law School. I, in turn, attended the University of South Carolina, working part time as a telephone operator with the South Carolina State Law Enforcement Division (SLED). Following separate career paths resulted in our having little if any contact for several years. We reunited later through David's employment as an assistant solicitor, prosecuting criminal cases in Dillon County and my role as a criminal investigator with SLED. Our reconnection led to an ongoing personal friendship that continues to this day. David later left the solicitor's office to enter private law practice, and I retired from SLED to answer a call to pastoral ministry in the United Methodist Church. Over the years leading up to this, David had suffered personal tragedies in his life that left him with no family. His mother died in 1975, and his older brother and father died four months apart in 1983. Notwithstanding the emotional pain and suffering involved, David persevered, knowing that his life had a much greater purpose for which he had been prepared.

The episode with the sprinkler that morning in March 2014 marked what would become a turning point in David's life. In addition to having no sensation or stimuli from the water and having noticed from a self-examination a large tumor in the area of his right breast, David soon met with his family physician, who initially suspected a diagnosis of breast cancer. A referral and later examination by a surgeon, who ordered a series of medical tests and scans, confirmed the diagnosis, with David having five of the seven symptoms of breast cancer. A subsequent surgery—a double mastectomy—was successful, but the recovery time would progress slowly with comprehensive regimens of follow-up treatments. In one such treatment regimen, David endured serious blood-circulation complications from a round of chemotherapy, resulting in the amputation of part of his right foot. Over the ensuing time from his initial diagnosis in April 2014 to April two years later, David had eight surgical procedures. He was told prior to some of the procedures that his chances of not waking up were greater than of his waking, but David was someone of great personal resolve and determination.

One day, not long after David's mastectomy, I had the opportunity to visit with him while he was a patient at a nearby hospital. I mark this day as the date on which our relationship grew even stronger. We had a cordial visit that eventually turned into how God was working in David's life. He had a remarkably optimistic attitude, considering what he had been through. I continued to stay in contact with him regarding his health and healing.

One day I received a telephone call at my home. It was David asking if I could accompany him to Florence for a disability hearing. David's specialty in his law practice is representing clients who are seeking disability compensation. He related that he was currently on a knee scooter and would be unable to both mobilize himself and carry a large briefcase into the federal courthouse. Without hesitation, I offered to go. This was the first of several opportunities I had to accompany David to his scheduled hearings. The conversations we had during these times were sometimes light-hearted (David had his own unique sense of humor) and sometimes spiritually uplifting. We searched our hearts as we shared about David's health and his current condition. One afternoon as we rode along, I said, "David, think about it. As a lawyer representing clients who are disabled, you are now disabled yourself. Where you once worked *for* disabled people, you are now working *with* them as one who is disabled."

David acknowledged this and replied, "Paul, I could have retired on disability, but that is not what I am here for. I am going to continue this work as long as I can." David was healed and restored in order to better understand the very clients he represented. His status as an advocate had changed due to his breast cancer and the treatments that followed. David did not resign himself to a life of pity. Once he was able, he continued to work tirelessly for his clients. David now had a new perspective on his work; his role as an advocate offered his clients a renewed sense of hope. The Spirit of God breaking into David's life through his cancer had given him a new identity and refined his faith profoundly, enabling David to see his role as a lawyer in a completely new way. A friend once asked him, "David, if you could put into one sentence what all this has meant to you, what would you say?"

David said without hesitation, "Before all this, I thought I knew who I was, but I was mistaken." David could say without reservation, "Yes, Lord, You know that I love You." With this love, David was able to attend to the needs of those whom God had sent his way. "Tend my sheep" (John 21:16b). The voice of Christ resonated deeply with David's spirit, even in those times when he was not consciously aware of it.

CHAPTER 13

Divine Appointments

I am sometimes taken aback by the people who come into my life at what appear to be strategic times. Over the years, I have tried to perceive these situations as God's way of speaking to me in some way, opening my heart to a new understanding of Him and His presence around me. What I have failed to discern in all of this is how God puts even dogs in our path to open up opportunities for ministry! Such a situation happened for Laura and me a few years ago. Laura had returned to the classroom as an elementary teacher after nine years in pastoral ministry. I was serving two churches in Marlboro County near the North Carolina state line. A couple of times each month, we would leave home late on a Friday afternoon and spend that night at our family cottage in North Myrtle Beach. We would return home the following afternoon so I could prepare for the Sunday worship services. The highlight of our twenty-four-hour stay was often the time we spent on the beach early on Saturday mornings, usually shortly after daybreak. Many times, Laura would walk a mile or so down the strand while I loafed in my beach chair, reading, watching the waves come and go, or simply contemplating how much older I had become.

One particular Saturday morning stands out in our memories. Laura and I had walked down to the ocean about three blocks from our small cottage. We found a spot to set up our beach chairs and settled in for an hour or so. I must add that Laura loves animals of all kinds. I have told people, jokingly of course, that she would have a giraffe in the house if it would fit. Every time we pass a flock of goats near the highway, I have to slow down so she can look at them. But her real affinity is for dogs, every breed of dog. Whether it is in a parking lot, a pet shop, a street fair, wherever, she always has to pet any dog that comes our way. Years ago, we traveled to Colorado on vacation and happened to be in the town of Breckenridge. We had been visiting some of the shops there when a couple of dogs passed where we were walking. "Oh, what sweet dogs," I can just hear her saying all these years later. "Here, doggie, doggie," she said as she drew closer. In an effort to befriend the dogs, Laura, in her animated way, barked gently at the dogs. "Ruff! Ruff!" Surprisingly, one of them barked back and "gestured" in a not-so-friendly way. Sensing this might not be the most pleasant experience of our trip, we quickly found our way into another shop nearby.

As for this particular morning on the beach, Laura and I found a suitable place on the strand far enough away that the incoming tide would not wash over us. We enjoy meeting and occasionally talking to people passing by our spot, asking them where they are from and getting to know more about them. We have met some very interesting people this way. On this morning, we noticed a man walking in our direction with a dog on a leash. As he came near us, Laura stood up to ask if she could pet the Brittany Spaniel, who, we soon learned, was named Samantha. We exchanged introductions, spoke briefly, and soon our conversation turned to occupations. We learned that the man and his wife had spent their working years in the public school system in North Carolina, serving as teachers and school principals. An immediate connection was made, as Laura had spent many years serving as an elementary school teacher. This "divine appointment," as I would soon come to define it, led to a wonderful ongoing friendship with Michael and Linda Donnell from North Carolina. Very likely, he would have passed us by with only the slightest of greetings had it not been for my wife's love for dogs—and a precious Brittany Spaniel named Samantha.

Later, Laura and I met Michael's wife, Linda, and we planned to have dinner one night at a local restaurant in North Myrtle Beach. The time we had that night gave us the opportunity to get to know one another. As we spoke openly about our personal lives, it soon became obvious that we all shared much in common. Laura, Michael, and Linda had a glorious time exchanging experiences in their roles as teachers, and Michael and Linda as principals in the public school systems. All of us were members of small United Methodist churches. Laura and I had served as pastors. Laura had since returned to the classroom after nine years in pastoral ministry, and I was still serving two churches in Marlboro County, South Carolina. This first delightful meal together granted us the feeling that this was a friendship that was meant to be. Only in the weeks that followed did I come to realize how the light of God's grace would shine even brighter on our friendship and what awaited me.

The occasion was another meal with Michael and Linda at a local Italian restaurant. We exchanged pleasantries and caught up on the events of one another's lives since our last meeting. At some point in our conversation, I mentioned that I had recently served on a mission team to Rwanda in Africa. The topic of Africa piqued Linda's attention, as the church she and Michael attended was supporting one of the Lost Boys of Sudan.

Sudan—Darfur, in the Sudan! As a United Methodist minister in 2007, I attended our denomination's annual conference, held in Florence, South Carolina, the first week of June. On the third day of the conference, a resolution came before the conference, dealing with the crisis in Darfur. I must confess that until that time, I had been somewhat oblivious to events in Darfur. Having limited knowledge of the Darfur crisis and even less of its full implications, coupled with my being removed geographically rendered me apathetic at best. Regrettably, my apathy and indifference grew out of an attitude that it did not involve me because the issue was in an area far removed from our culture and country. I certainly did not feel that anything I did, if ever led to do so, could make a difference. Secondly, perhaps the media coverage concerning the atrocities in Darfur was inadequate in informing the American public on the depth and extent of human suffering. In the midst of a civil war in Sudan, close to a half million people had died by that time, with countless others driven from their homes to live in sordid refugee camps. The South Carolina annual conference that year passed a resolution calling for an end to the atrocities and respect for the dignity of human life.

A couple of weeks later, my wife and I were at a bookstore in Myrtle Beach, South Carolina, (one of our greatest weaknesses, of course). I was browsing through the current-events section and turned to look at the shelf behind me. When I did, it was as if my eyes were trained on a book on the second shelf. The book was not in a place for all the customers to see, as is done when the store is promoting a certain book. One had to really be looking to see this particular one. The title of the book was *Not on Our Watch* by Don Cheadle and John Prendergast. Having recalled the action taken previously at our annual conference, I pulled the book down and thumbed through it. It looked interesting, and I could not help but be captivated by what I saw in the pictures and what the captions noted. Up until this time, I had no real interest or concern about the situation in Darfur. For some compelling reason, I felt that I needed to learn more about this crisis. So I purchased the book.

In reading *Not on Our Watch*, I was mesmerized by the despicable plight and incomprehensible suffering of the people of Darfur. This book was very informative, thought-provoking, and a troubling account of human suffering that served to transform my attitude toward those whose lives are utterly hopeless and in desperate need of political intervention. Having read this book, I felt compelled to take the time to write South Carolina's US senators and all six members of Congress concerning this issue and urge their support in taking the necessary action to alleviate the human suffering and prevent future injustices in these regions. I wrote the letter on September 10, 2007. It is inconceivable to think that one could read *Not on Our Watch* and not be moved to act in some way. On a later occasion, I telephoned the South Carolina governor's office to voice my support of a divestiture bill concerning investments in Sudan that had been passed by the South Carolina legislature and was being presented to Governor Mark Sanford for signature or veto. The divestiture bill eventually passed, thanks to the outpouring support of so many concerned people.

Michael and Linda knew nothing at our dinner meeting that night about my interest in the people of Darfur in Sudan. I could hardly believe what I was hearing! Suddenly, the resolution at annual conference in 2007, the books I had read about the genocidal atrocities in Darfur, and the active stance I had taken in contacting members of Congress were taking on a new life for me. As our conversation continued, Linda noticed my interest in the sufferings of the Sudanese people, which eventually paved the way for my having the opportunity later to connect with Jacob, one of the Lost Boys of Sudan. *What!* I thought to myself. Because of a chance encounter on the beach, I was being presented with the possibility of getting acquainted with a young man from Sudan who had lived and experienced what I had only read and learned about.

Linda later introduced us to Roger Paxton, a pastor, and his wife, Nancy, who were captivated by what they had witnessed on a weekly news segment regarding the Lost Boys of Sudan and felt the need to get involved in some way. Roger began searching the internet for ways to do this. After several months of internet research, and through his eventual connection with an organization supporting the Lost Boys, his efforts paid off. It was through my subsequent conversation with Roger and the information provided to me that I was able to contact an individual whom I will refer to as Jacob.

In the two and a half years that Laura and I were acquainted with Jacob, our conversations were by telephone. During this time, Jacob, along with several other Sudanese men, was enrolled at a school of theology in Pittsburgh, Pennsylvania. We spoke with him several times a year, often about his academic work, his family back in Sudan, and his wife and children who were living with a family in Australia at that time. He wanted desperately to reconnect with them once he completed his ministerial studies.

There were poignant moments when Jacob would relate to us the hardships of fleeing Sudan and what they encountered along the way. He also spoke of the difficulties of getting adjusted to life in the United States. As I did not make notes of the details of our conversations, much of what Jacob shared has eluded me over time.

Jacob also educated me on what life was like for his family back in Sudan. They often had to travel for hours in order to buy food, supplies and other provisions for their essential needs. It became evident that the welfare of his family in Sudan always concerned Jacob. He invariably asked me to pray for his family that they would be able to get all that was needed to sustain them. Jacob and I also had occasions to talk about scripture. He shared with me that the Cushites in the Old Testament were the ancestors of the present-day Sudanese people.

One day I received a call from Jacob advising me that his family in Sudan was in dire straits and needed to rent some cows in order to fertilize the land they had. Without this, the land would not have the adequate nourishment to raise their crops. He asked that I pray that they would be able to have the money to rent the cows. "How much would it cost to rent the cows, Jacob?" I asked. "Two hondred feefty dullas for thutty days," he said in his African accent. I loved listening to Jacob talk. One can only imagine how this conversation progressed across cultural lines. "Ween thay manooa dry, they brek it op, spred eet owt, and plow eet ehn. Lahnd thayn gaytt fehtilized," he plainly stated. After hearing more about this, I sensed that we would need to help Jacob's family, although he never asked for money, only prayers. Jacob was never a burden in this regard. After agreeing to help Jacob's family, we spoke for a few more minutes and ended the conversation. I told Laura afterward about our conversation, and she could not help but laugh. "Those people sure have a way of getting by, don't they?" she said.

As time passed, Jacob continued to stay in contact with us and update us on his academic work, his family concerns, and plans he had following graduation, which he really looked forward to. He was scheduled to graduate in May 2011. He had hoped to return to Seattle for a while and eventually reunite with his wife and children in Australia.

In April 2011, Laura and I received an envelope in the mail from Jacob. Praise God! The card we received that day was an invitation to Jacob's graduation from the Trinity School of Ministry, to be held at the Trinity Episcopal Cathedral in Pittsburgh on Saturday, May 14. We planned to attend and were excited about finally getting to meet Jacob.

Laura and I were very amused at their usage of the English language. One day while we were having lunch with Jacob and some of the others at a restaurant in Pittsburgh, one of Jacob's roommates remarked about something they need to do by four o'clock. Someone across the table seated next to me looked at his watch and said, "Four is already gone." Laura and I would have said, "Well, it's after four now." But our Sudanese brother said, "Four is already gone," as if to say, "four is already gone and you ain't gonna get it back," to use our southern vernacular. But what could I say? I tried to get Jacob to teach me a few phrases in Dinka, a dialect of their native language. Needless to say, Jacob did not have a teachable student to work with. Jacob and his Sudanese brothers were doing better with English than I could ever hope to do with Dinka.

Another instance came when we were on our way to a luncheon across town, following the graduation ceremony. A local church had prepared a Sudanese meal for the graduates and their families. I was driving with Laura seated on the front passenger side and Jacob and his wife in the back seat. For some reason, we ended up going the wrong way and tried to find a place to turn around. If you have never been with me when I get lost or stuck in traffic with any kind of deadline or appointment to make, you are blessed not to be there. I looked for several places to turn around before I was ever able to do so. Once I did, Jacob said, "We in a good way now. We in a good way."

I never heard back from Jacob after he moved to Seattle following his graduation. I can honestly say that my experience with him, learning of his life struggles and connecting across distant cultural boundaries through Christ as Lord was a genuine blessing in my life. There were great faith lessons to be gleaned in my two-and-a-half-year relationship with Jacob.

CHAPTER 14

Lost, Found, and Found Again

In those times when we consider the people God has put in our lives during the course of our faith journey—those who come into our path unexpectedly for reasons we are not aware of at the time—we often fail to take into account people from years past. Such encounters may have preceded the time when we surrendered our life to the lordship of Jesus Christ and were not necessarily attuned to God's presence. God's purpose in these times may not have been for the particular person in need but instead may have been for those individuals whose concerted efforts addressed the need. Reflecting on those former times has the potential of calling to our minds how God was there, even when we did not sense His presence.

To some people, the events that began on the afternoon of Friday, June 5, 1998, would hardly be considered a big deal. Personally, I still recall the experience with a great sense of personal satisfaction. More so from a ministry perspective, reflecting on what transpired that one week twenty years ago lends even greater meaning.

The telephone rang at my home on that afternoon. The caller was Tommy Coleman, a friend of mine from our hometown of

Latta. Knowing that I worked with the State Law Enforcement Division, Tommy asked if he could come by our house. He had something he wanted to show me and wasn't quite sure what to do with it. Minutes later, Tommy arrived, sat down with me, and showed me a wallet that he had found on the highway in Florence. He explained that he was en route home from visiting with a friend in Timmonsville, South Carolina. As Tommy turned left off of US Highway 76 onto the exit ramp that proceeds up to the northbound lane of Interstate 95, his attention was drawn to an object on the side of the road. The manner in which the object was flipped open revealed what appeared to be identification cards of some sort. Tommy backed up his vehicle and got out to further examine what the object might be. In doing so, he found a wallet with cash and identification cards, indicating that it belonged apparently to a foreign exchange student. As we pored through the contents of the wallet that afternoon, we found a student identification card for a Heike Franziska Jürrens. Tommy asked if I thought I might be able to locate the owner, as the wallet contained important information that the owner would not want to lose. He left the wallet with me, and I assured him I would do whatever I could to find the owner.

In my capacity as a law-enforcement officer, my first inclination, of course, was of the welfare of the owner of the wallet. Hopefully, the information found in the wallet would eventually lead me to the owner, who would be found safe. I contacted several law-enforcement agencies in the area, inquiring as to anyone having reported a missing lady's wallet. No reports had been made. I then called the Criminal Intelligence Division at SLED headquarters for any assistance they could render in locating the family of the person listed on the student identification card found in the wallet. I managed to identify what we believed to be a telephone and a fax number from the card. A faxed message was sent to a number that appeared to be a school in Germany. SLED Intelligence also called the German Embassy here in the United States and the American Embassy in Munich, Germany, explaining how the wallet was found and that we were attempting to locate the owner or her family. We also shared our concern about the welfare of the owner. To our dismay, one embassy advised that we would have to call back on Monday, and the other said that they couldn't make those kinds of decisions. Dottie Cronise of SLED Intelligence also called directory assistance for Germany through an overseas MCI operator, seeking help in getting a call through to the telephone number found on the student ID. She and I called the number several times throughout the weekend, all to no avail.

My arrival at the regional SLED office on Monday, June 8, was met with a promising development. A fax had come into the office over the weekend from the school in Germany with an address and telephone number for Heike Franziska Jürrens's mother in Germany. I called the school in Germany and advised that we had received their fax. An employee of the school with whom I spoke expressed her appreciation for what was being done to locate Heike, and she, likewise, was concerned about her. The employee had also tried repeatedly to locate Heike's mother but was also unable to find her. I called this number from Monday to Wednesday with no success. Still I wondered about this young lady. *How was she? Where was she?* There was no evidence that a crime had occurred concerning this matter.

I had grown increasingly frustrated over the past two days by our inability to locate Heike. Earlier on Wednesday, I traveled to Conway and Sumter, South Carolina, on unrelated business, arriving back at the regional office in Effingham about three o'clock that afternoon. As I took a seat at the desk in my office, I felt the urge to try calling Heike's mother one more time. I dialed the number and waited patiently in that brief customary pause when an overseas connection is being made. Riiiiing! *(No answer.)* Riiiiing! *(No answer.)* Riiiiing! On the third ring, and much to my surprise, someone answered. Having no idea how "hello" is spoken in German, but recognizing the voice of a woman on the other end of the line, I asked if she spoke English. She could but very little. I tried with much difficulty to explain what had happened, my purpose for calling. She managed with some difficulty to understand the words *daughter* and *money* and sensed that the call had something to do with her daughter. She then asked to speak to her daughter, thinking her daughter was there with me. Unable to get her to understand, it immediately became apparent from the frantic tone of her voice that she thought her daughter might have been kidnapped and this was a ransom call. I tried my best to calm her and get her to understand. She was frantic, almost to the point of hysteria. I then said "police, police," and she understood. Slowly regaining her composure, she began to understand that the police in the United States needed to contact her daughter. She gave me a telephone number for Heike in Spring Valley, New York. With her limited English, I had difficulty understanding the number but managed to get it. I was elated. Our efforts had paid off.

I immediately called the number given me for Heike in New York. A young man whom I will refer to as Quentin answered. I identified myself and explained to him my purpose for calling. He said the number I had called was an elderly-care facility in Spring Valley. He acknowledged that he knew Heike and that he had last talked to her the day before. I now knew that she was all right and that all we had to deal with at this point was a missing wallet. He advised that he would try to locate her and have her call me. I asked Quentin to also have Heike call her mother in Germany to allay her fears and to relate to her what had happened. Minutes later, Quentin called me back, advising that Heike had gone to Manhattan for the day and would be back around seven o'clock. I furnished my home telephone number and asked that he have her call me later that night. I also explained to Quentin how upset her mother was and the difficulty I had communicating with her. Quentin advised that there was someone there at the center who spoke fluent German. *What? Brush it off, Paul! This is no coincidence.*

I had to stop momentarily and take this all in. At this point, it became evident that God's hand was in this in a mighty way. After all, I had asked a few of my friends to pray that we would locate the owner of the wallet and find her safe. I asked Quentin to have that person call Heike's mother. A few minutes after hanging up, I felt that perhaps I should call Quentin back and ask him to let me know when they had spoken to Heike's mother, so I would have the satisfaction of knowing that she was all right. When I called back, a young lady answered, who advised that she had just spoken to Heike's mother and that everything was fine. *Praise God for having someone at the center who spoke fluent German.*

At some point during this day, we received a fax from the school in Germany, advising that Heike's mother was off for holidays that week and would not be back at work until Monday, June 15. She advised that she would keep trying to get in touch with her. Upon seeing this fax, I felt that I should inform the school that we had located Heike. They were elated upon hearing the news.

That afternoon, I arrived home from work at six o'clock. I called my friend Tommy to let him know that we had located Heike and that I was expecting her to call me around seven that night. I asked him if he wanted to speak to her when she called. If so, I could conference him in. He said he certainly wanted to.

I could hardly wait to hear that voice. We had come a long way, crossing many hurdles from where we originally started with this matter, wondering if foul play had been involved. The call we had waited for came at seven fifteen that Wednesday night, June 10. Her accent alone thrilled me. I regret that I did not record the call. The joy in her voice made all of the efforts worthwhile. I tried to conference Tommy in on the call, but he was not at home. While I continued to speak with Heike on the phone, a friend of ours came to the house to bring our daughter Lauren home from softball practice. My wife went out to meet with her. As she did, Tommy and his wife, Gayle, happened to pass by the house and waved. Laura quickly motioned for them to come inside. Noting Laura's excitement, they drove into the driveway. Laura shared with them that I was on the phone with Heike at that time. Tommy immediately came into the house and spoke with her. *(God had Tommy in the right place at just the right time. Yes, He is in this.)* Heike's exuberance became our hallelujahs.

Now, all that remained would be to get the wallet back to Heike. She told us to keep the money if she could just get her wallet with her personal information returned to her. We assured her that she would get it all back intact, and I arranged to mail the wallet back to her in Germany.

The next day, June 11, I met with Chuck Mackey, the postmaster of the Latta Post Office, with the wallet, and shared this story with him. I inquired about mailing the wallet and its contents to Germany. I told Chuck that the owner was scheduled to leave for her home in Germany on June 14. Chuck related his concerns about mailing the wallet internationally, especially with the cash it contained.

"What should we do, Chuck? Do we have time to get it to her before she leaves?" I asked.

"We'll have to mail it by overnight express mail, Paul," Chuck said. "Can you call her and get her address in New York? Do you have a number for her?"

"Yes, I do. I'll call her."

I called Heike back in New York to get an address where to mail the package. Chuck wrapped the wallet in a secure package and mailed it, marked for Overnight Express Mail, to Heike's address in New York. Chuck was so caught up in the excitement of it all that he personally paid for the postage. On Friday, June 12, Chuck called the postal authorities in New York three times to stress the importance of getting the package delivered. One attempt was made that morning at eleven thirty but was unsuccessful. He called later and was advised that the package had been delivered at 3:00 p.m. That afternoon, just prior to my leaving the office in Effingham for home, I received a telephone call from Heike, advising that she had received her wallet. Heike was ecstatic to the point of tears, not expecting that she would ever see her money or the wallet with its contents again. Shortly after receiving her wallet, Heike shared what had happened with her friends, her teachers here in the United States, and her teachers in Germany.

Sometime later, I received a letter of appreciation from Heike with a beautiful piece of handwritten artwork done by her, which I still have in my possession today. I also received a personal note from the school in Germany. Both letters were expressions of deep gratitude for all that had been done by so many people to get Heike's wallet returned to her.

I have shared this story for two reasons. First, the story is not primarily about a missing wallet but about people, the compassionate hearts of people from a small town in South Carolina to a college town in Germany to an elderly-care facility in Spring Valley, New York. People in pursuit of a common goal and whose efforts transcended geographical mind-sets and cultural differences to assist a young woman in need. Such diligent strivings served the ends of what was good, right, honorable, noble, and trustworthy.

Secondly, and most importantly, the heartfelt response I received from Heike upon having her wallet returned intact nourished my soul in ways that praise, accolades, or awards never could have. The excitement in her voice when she called our home that afternoon to offer me and the others her gratitude for what had been done for her will always stand as an indelible memory. I believe I would have understood every word even if she had spoken in German! My hope is that the same would have been done if this were our daughter in the same situation in Germany. This episode occurred one year prior to my retiring from SLED in May 1999 to enter pastoral ministry. Could this event and how I witnessed it unfold and come to fruition have been an incremental step in what I will always consider a call by God on my life that began years before? For now, it all may be what I see in a mirror dimly, but I may come to know for certain when God wills to reveal it to me.

CHAPTER 15

Time to Consider

"Do you love me?" Jesus asked Simon Peter a third time (John 21:17). Biblical tradition holds that the three times Jesus asked Simon son of John if he loved Jesus coincided with Peter's three denials of Jesus after Jesus's arrest. With this in mind, two significant points can be made in the third denial of Peter. The synoptic gospels, Matthew, Mark, and Luke, indicate that there was a lapse in time before the second and the third denial. Matthew (26:73) and Mark (14:70) state that "after a little while" Peter was confronted about his being "one of them" (Mark 14:70, Matthew 26:73) who had been with Jesus. Luke in his gospel says that "A little later" (Luke 22:58) and "Then about an hour later" (22:59) Peter was accused of being with Jesus. Did Peter have sufficient time to consider what he had done? I cannot escape the fact that in my own life there are times, those introspective intervals, when I must consider how I have betrayed Christ; how I have essentially denied Him by my words or my actions, strayed from Him by seeking my own way in life, following my own desires and ambitions, or even dishonoring Him.

Secondly, all three gospels relate that it was Peter's manner of speech, his accent, that led the others to believe that he was a Galilean and therefore a follower who had accompanied Jesus. I am led to consider what distinctive characteristics others may see in us that identify us as Christians.

CONCLUSION

The Lessons Learned

One day toward the latter stages of my initial draft of this book, I prayed, as I often did, for God's guidance in the thoughts I needed to convey. As my journal entry of three years ago dealt with my envisioning being with Jesus that day and His posing to me the question "Do you love Me?", in my prayer, another vague image formed recently in my mind. I imagined myself taking a seat at a table where sat Willie Nettles, David Watson, Jacob, and Heike Jürrens. I looked around the table with a deep sense of wonderment and gratitude for the people God had put into my life. Each person sat silently with his or her own unique personality and characteristics, from diverse walks of life, with very little in common. One found himself trapped in a life of substance abuse for years, another was in the throes of a life-threatening illness, a third fled the atrocities of a civil war, and a fourth I had never met or known anything about personally. Please do not construe this as a label I am placing on these individuals but instead as my way of revealing how God works in the lives of people, some whom we least expect, or through their respective situations to teach significant faith lessons.

I chose none of these people on my own. God by His all-sufficient grace put them in my life at strategic times because He had something to teach me through them. As I envisioned each one, I began to realize that his or her particular life struggle represented a part of my life. I look back at the passage from Ephesians chapter 2, wherein Paul writes, "But God, who is rich in mercy, out of the great love with which he loved us even when we were dead through our trespasses, made us alive together with Christ" (Ephesians 2:4–5a). Was there some area of my life that God needed to redeem, to bring back to life through each of these people? I have no doubt that there was. Would this be the impetus from which we would form a common bond, alive together with Christ? By all means! This represented an *even when* moment in my life.

What might God's purpose have been in bringing us together? Again, I turn to a key phrase in the Ephesians passage—*so that* (2:7). Paul writes, "so that in the ages to come he might show the immeasurable riches of his grace in kindness toward us in Christ Jesus." We can never lose sight of how, in feeding the lambs of Christ in the world around us, in tending to and feeding his people, two critical truths are opened to our understanding. First, in our kindness toward one another, we are following the example of Christ in His kindness toward us. We experience spiritual sustenance and nourishment for our own lives in the very people to whom God calls us. Secondly, as we discern spiritually the giving and receiving in such situations, we get a glimpse of God's heavenly kingdom. The purpose for all Christians is to witness to the riches of God's grace by loving others as He has loved us.

So how did I receive the spiritual sustenance needed for my faith journey through these four people? These faith lessons did not come immediately. They came only in a way and at a time that enabled me to understand their true significance for my life. I continued to gain understanding even in the writing of this book. Above all, I praise God for putting these people in my life at His appointed time. To Him be the glory and the honor and the praise.

WILLIE NETTLES

We all have those people who have crossed our path in life and caused us to stop and take an honest look at ourselves, to search our hearts deeply and reflect on what this person's life has meant to us. This becomes a discipline in seriously considering what is most important in life and who we are living for. In some instances, I have found that such times are most evident for me during the person's funeral service. What can I glean from that person's life that could make me a better person? It was my misfortune to have known Willie personally for only two and a half years. But the bond we shared was invaluable.

Living alone can be a real struggle for many people, especially for someone recovering from drug and alcohol addiction. The temptation constantly seeks a chink in one's armor, a weakness into which the temptation can enter and take hold. In reflecting on Willie's life at the time I knew him, I am reminded of the teaching of Jesus from the Gospel of Luke (Luke 11:24–26):

> When the unclean spirit has gone out of a person, it wanders through waterless regions looking for a resting place, but not finding any, it says, "I will return to my house from which I came." When it comes, it finds it swept and put in order. Then it goes and brings seven other spirits more evil than itself, and they enter and live there; and the last state of that person is worse than the first.

Willie did not leave his "house" empty, but he put something in place of the addiction from which he had been delivered. Willie's early-morning text messages to the many friends who were fortunate to receive them reminded us of the intentional devotional life Willie immersed himself in. He treasured his solitude and his time alone with God. Physically, Willie lived mostly by himself; however, he knew deep within his spirit that he was never alone.

Willie also enjoyed and valued the many people in his life, both past and present and from all walks of life. The text messages bear witness to this. One day as Willie and I were traveling to Florence for an appointment he had, he mentioned the many people he saw at the home of Mrs. Eloise Smith, whose funeral was held a couple of days earlier. Mrs. Eloise was like a mother to so many young people over the years. She possessed a true spirit and a gift for hospitality, and her home and family had become a safe haven for Willie in those troubled years of his past. Willie saw many of his high school classmates at the gathering in Mrs. Eloise's home after the funeral that he had not seen in years. I could sense how much this meant to Willie by the way he spoke so cheerfully about it.

Willie never demonstrated the materialistic attitude that is so evident in our world today. The advertising industry has beset our culture with choices that would have us believe that certain items will enhance the quality of our lives. Certainly, this is true in some respects. But the choices we sometimes make do not always fulfill the desires of our hearts. So we have to acquire more or look elsewhere to obtain the satisfaction we so desperately want. A materialistic culture is driven by two compelling forces. One is the desire for something else more meaningful to better serve our needs. This is apparent in one's search for a new job with more satisfaction or in a situation where one spouse wants out of a marriage because he or she has found someone else who can bring a greater sense of physical and emotional satisfaction. Secondly, there is the desire for more: more money, more clothes, a new house, another car, when nothing else is needed. It all comes down to something else or something more. Want begets want.

So how does one find contentment in such a self-driven,

materialistic, competitive, and greedy culture? Going back to the words of the psalmist: "The LORD is my shepherd" (Psalm 23:1), I truly believe that this was Willie's greatest desire, implicit in his last text message to me. Willie, like all of us, struggled with personal issues in his life, but his struggle was not a quest for more. Willie longed to be restored to the person God created him to be, to hear deep within his spirit that still, small voice saying to him, "All's well, Willie, all is well."

Willie served up valuable lessons from which we all can find spiritual sustenance for a continuing faith journey. On April 14, 2017, four months after Willie's death, his niece Leeanne found a note in a Bible her mom had given her for her birthday several years earlier. The note read:

Dearest Leeanne,
This is God's letter to you. Study it and read it often as you can. Eternity is your future. I love you. Uncle Willie.

The note was dated July 19, 2013. From her early youth up until her high school years, Leeanne enjoyed no real meaningful relationship with her uncle Willie. Even at an early age, she felt awkward around him because of his unusual behavior. Leeanne attributed this emotional distance and strain in their relationship to Willie's alcohol abuse. Following Leeanne's graduation from high school, Willie had returned from Wyoming, where he had spent four years working and attending a small college, working toward a college degree. Upon his return, Willie had found employment in a nearby business where Leeanne and her mother, Pearl, would visit with him occasionally. A year later, following Willie's release from the Dillon County Jail, Leeanne began to notice a difference in Willie's demeanor. Something had changed in his life. Their relationship slowly evolved into what Leeanne had always hoped it would be—loving, congenial, and supportive. The note Leeanne found in her Bible on that day in April 2017 enabled her to see what had formed the basis for their renewed relationship. God's Word had opened Willie's heart to another relationship that he so desperately needed for his own life—Jesus Christ. And now, "Uncle Willie" wanted for Leeanne what he had found in a personal relationship with his Lord. From this time forward, Leeanne began to sense her own need for a relationship with Jesus Christ as Lord and Savior.

The apostle Paul, in a letter to young Timothy, spoke these words: "The saying is sure and worthy of full acceptance, that Christ Jesus came into the world to save sinners—of whom I am the foremost. But for that very reason I received mercy, so that in me, as the foremost, Jesus Christ might display the utmost patience, making me an example to those who would come to believe in him for eternal life" (1 Timothy 1:15–16). Never would I even attempt to call Willie, or anyone else, for that matter, the worst of sinners, for I have a log in my own eye, as Jesus taught. But I learned from my time with Willie and all that he shared with me that a sinner's transformation in Christ can be the best example of the patience of Christ when that person comes to believe. This led me to reflect on my own life, grateful for the patience God has granted me in Christ Jesus when I strayed so far from Him. I further must live with the knowledge that the sanctifying work of the Holy Spirit is a work in progress in me daily.

I could feast on lessons learned from Willie's experience that our past is not our present and that true life is not found in wealth and possessions or in the counterfeit exhilarations of drugs and alcohol and their attendant pleasures. The true life is found in Jesus Christ, the Great Shepherd and the people through whom He comes to us and shapes us for His purposes.

DAVID WATSON

"Before all this, I thought I knew who I was, but I was mistaken."
This revelation David had about his ongoing bout with breast cancer resonates deeply with me. We have this human tendency to find our identity in three key areas. First is the people we know and with whom we associate closely; those with whom we work and spend quality time. When the level of trust deepens, valuable advice and guidance are sought in personal matters. Genuine acceptance for who we are and safe havens in times of trouble are certainly engendered.

There is also the issue of our careers. How often do we ask another person whom we have the opportunity to meet for the first time, "So where do you work? What do you do for a living?" The answer we get immediately forms an opinion about how we perceive that person. Whether the person is a teacher, a doctor, a janitor, a lawyer, a store clerk, a police officer, a factory worker, or what have you, we have a tendency to relate that person through that particular lens. That person takes on this identity by virtue of how others relate to her or him.

Of particular import in terms of identity is the family name. On those occasions when some of my friends see me, especially those from my high school graduating class, they will say "Gasque," with the first name going unmentioned. Thus, the family name is immediately identified. I have experienced this many times in various locations. I almost invariably call David "Mr. Watson," with the emphatic tone of voice often used by a renowned circuit judge in speaking to David in a courtroom session when David served as an assistant prosecuting attorney. Almost everyone attains a certain identity based on his or her background and family lineage. This is especially true when other people detect personal traits, mannerisms, and physical characteristics that our parents had. Our son, Conan, served for several years as a sports reporter and later as a sports anchor for a local television station in Myrtle Beach. A friend of ours who watched his broadcast would say to me or my wife at times, "Well, I saw Paul Gasque on TV last night," referring to how much Conan shared some of my mannerisms.

We humans derive our identity in a myriad of ways. But I cannot escape those words David shared with a friend and later with me about his cancer and how it altered his perception of who he was. For twenty-five years, I carried a badge and a gun in my profession as a law-enforcement officer. Many people identified me by the legal authority this granted me. Yes, there is a sense of pride and dignity that accompanies such a profession when the service is rendered with fairness, dignity, and integrity. But there is a hidden danger in when one usurps that authority through arrogance, egotism, and needless superiority. I have no doubt that I allowed myself to take on this attitude at times. I recall a statement a fellow agent made to me on the day I shared with the agents of our region that I was leaving SLED to enter pastoral ministry. That afternoon in late May 1999, he and I were alone in the conference room of the regional office shortly after lunch. Obviously, he had been considering the announcement I had made earlier about retiring from law enforcement for another calling. He said to me, "Captain, you know when you leave SLED, you won't be 'Captain Gasque' anymore."

I looked over at him and responded with two words, "I know." Two words—a response that obscured the underlying fear and anxiety of leaving a profession with which I felt so secure and familiar, to answer a calling not knowing what pastoral ministry might entail. I can honestly say that this was a moment in my life when the words of the apostle Paul, "walk by faith, not by sight,"

(2 Corinthians 5:7) became very real and personal for me. Two words that perhaps brought light to what David had said years later: Perhaps *I* thought *I* knew who *I* was all those years; but did *I* really know? The Holy Scripture says in Romans 8:28–29a, "We know that all things work together for good for those who love God, who are called according to his purpose. For those whom he foreknew he also predestined to be conformed to the image of his Son." Looking back, I truly feel as if my identity was being reshaped in the latter part of 1991 and 1992. Surely God knew me all those years. Was this the time when I was beginning to know Him? Only years later did I come to realize it.

As Christians, our identity in Christ Jesus is shaped and formed through suffering, as in our suffering and afflictions we are being conformed more and more into the likeness of the one who suffered on our behalf. David recalled the words spoken in the preacher's message one Sunday during a worship service at the church he attended in North Myrtle Beach, South Carolina. He described it as if the preacher were speaking directly to him. "Rejoice in hope, be patient in suffering, persevere in prayer" (Romans 12:12) came the words from Paul's letter to the Romans. The passage resounded deep within David's spirit as he contemplated how patient he had to be through his bout with cancer. Only the grace of God in Christ Jesus could have granted David the patience he needed to sustain him in this battle. David's revelation and the way in which he has discerned his experience with cancer have allowed me to look back on my own struggles in life and see them for God's shaping purposes; how the untimely death of my brother Robert in 1995 at the age of thirty-eight, the death of my mom in 2001 from Alzheimer's disease, the death of my sister Judy five months later in 2002, and the death of my dad in 2011 have shaped me spiritually.

Lastly, and most importantly, my experience with David taught me more than how one finds identity in relationships, careers, and family heritage. I learned through David's perseverance and determination that life's struggles and hardships should never be an obstacle to how God can use us or as a limitation we are tempted to place on ourselves. These setbacks can lead to even greater ways of serving that define who we truly are as God's chosen instrument to others in need. In the words of the Lord to Paul following Paul's plea to be set free from a tormenting thorn in the flesh, "My grace is sufficient for you, for power is made perfect in weakness" (2 Corinthians 12:9).

JACOB

We have a human tendency to gather around us or to associate with people with whom we share much in common. As I write these words, our son, Conan, and his fiancée, Laura, are putting together a guest list for their wedding four months from now. They will include on their list relatives, close personal friends, individuals from their current and former places of employment, and others. In everyday life, be it small groups or clubs, outdoor activities, dining at restaurants, vacation trips, or activities with our children, there is generally a common bond that draws people together. In my relationship with Jacob, no such bonds existed, only my interest in Africa. I had developed a keen interest in African culture during my years of theological study at the Duke Divinity Course of Study from 2001 to 2005. The Darfur Resolution presented and approved at the South Carolina Annual Conference in 2007 became the catalyst for my learning more about the suffering and atrocities of the people of Sudan. I read accounts of the Lost Boys of Sudan, thousands of young men who fled the region of Darfur in the midst of a civil war, fearing for their lives. Whole villages were burned, totally devastated. Sexual violence and rape were rampant, and existing wells were purposely contaminated so the local villagers would not have access to much-needed water. Starvation became a weapon of the assailants. Thousands of young boys fled the region with nothing but the clothes on their backs and mostly barefooted. Along the way, many lost their lives from lions and crocodiles and other vicious predators. Many others drowned.

Those who survived eventually made the thousand-mile journey to Ethiopia, only to be driven out later.

Leaving Ethiopia, thousands of the Lost Boys fled to Kenya and settled in a refugee camp there. Realizing that returning to Sudan was too dangerous for the Lost Boys with a civil war still ongoing, approximately 3,600 boys were later granted the right to resettle in the United States by the United States Department of State, working in conjunction with the United Nations Human Rights Council. I had nothing whatsoever in common with Jacob, nor could I possibly fathom in the least what his life experience had been.

One element present in my life, but prior to my learning about Jacob, eventually became instrumental in my relationship with him. In January 2009, I traveled to Rwanda in sub-Saharan Africa with ZOE Ministries, a child-empowerment ministry of the United Methodist Church. ZOE was active in several nations in eastern Africa, partnering with local African officials and spiritual leaders to provide relief assistance to children orphaned by HIV/AIDS. The teams shared the love of Christ by providing the essential needs of food, clothing, education, and medical care. One significant emphasis of ZOE involved the child-empowerment program, which trained orphaned children in income-generating activities that would enable them to become independent and self-sufficient. Woven through all of this were the faith components of prayer, emotional and physical healing, and the gospel of Jesus Christ. During my time in Rwanda, I had the opportunity to witness what I had only previously read and heard about. I found it fascinating to interact with the people, to be a recipient of their gracious attitude, and to worship with them.

I recall having once read (although I have no recollection where I read it) of looking at someone's hands who had been through catastrophic life situations. What stories might those hands tell us? So as I sat with the others at the hamburger restaurant in Pittsburgh on the day of Jacob's graduation, I took the liberty of looking closely at the hands of our Sudanese friends there with us. *What stories might those hands tell me? What had they endured?*

What hope did those hands hold out for a better life, not knowing where they might find it?

I recall the passage from John's gospel where Jesus suddenly appeared to His disciples on the evening of His resurrection. The doors to the place where the disciples were hiding away had been locked for fear that, if found, they might endure the same cruel death as Jesus. The scripture reads, "Jesus came and stood among them and said, 'Peace be with you.' After he said this, he showed them his hands and his side. Then the disciples rejoiced when they saw the Lord" (John 20:19b–20). Jesus showed them His hands—hands that bore the scars of the redemptive work for the salvation of humankind; hands that gave us the freedom offered to us in Christ Jesus.

God had a purpose in bringing Jacob into my life at such a time. It was not Jacob's eyes that were opened throughout this experience but mine.

As I reflect on what I know of the struggles of the Lost Boys of Sudan, I think of their perseverance in following the vision of a better life—a life of hope and promise. Their willingness to take the chance of "making it." So I am left with two questions: *What in my life have I given up on that, had I persisted, would have led to a life-altering experience? Or am I in a struggle now calling for great perseverance?* We all need a Jacob, someone appointed by God to reveal to us the hope beyond what we can see; the determination to press on regardless of the circumstances, "looking to Jesus the pioneer and perfecter of our faith" (Hebrews 12:2); our hope of a spiritual breakthrough. A daybreak.

HEIKE JÜRRENS

Some might say, "Why, that was such a nice thing those people did for the young lady from Germany." Others might view it merely as law-enforcement authorities doing their job. "Isn't this what they are supposed to do?" some might ask. Still others might think, "Well, it was just a wallet with some money, a couple of identification cards, and other personal information. We all lose money on occasion. And the personal information can be replaced. What's the big deal? Aren't there far more critical cases they should be focusing on?" Yes, this is all true. But it is far more than any of this, as a letter I received from Heike the following month will reveal.

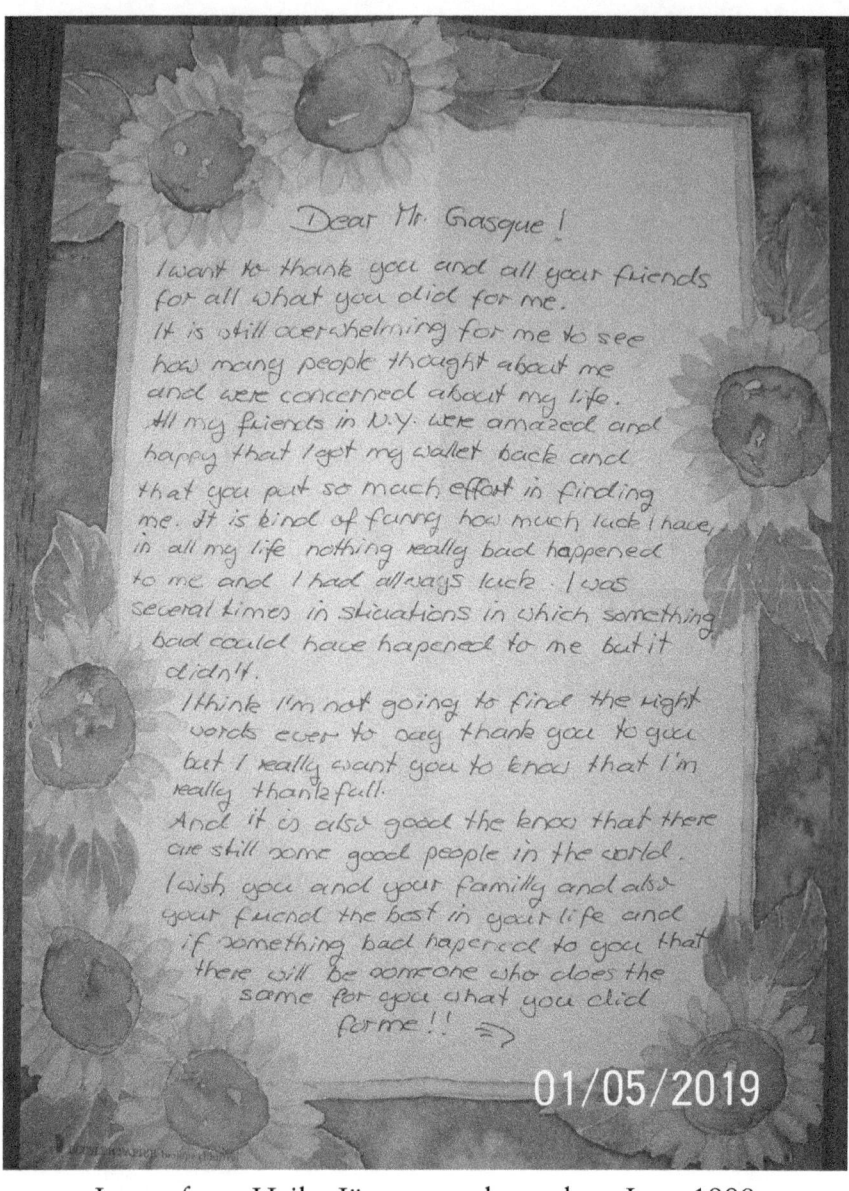

Dear Mr. Gasque!

I want to thank you and all your friends for all what you did for me.

It is still overwhelming for me to see how many people thought about me and were concerned about my life.

All my friends in N.Y. were amazed and happy that I got my wallet back and that you put so much effort in finding me. It is kind of funny how much luck I have, in all my life nothing really bad happened to me and I had always luck. I was several times in situations in which something bad could have happened to me but it didn't.

I think I'm not going to find the right words ever to say thank you to you but I really want you to know that I'm really thankfull.

And it is also good the know that there are still some good people in the world.

I wish you and your family and also your fuend the best in your life and if something bad happened to you that there will be someone who does the same for you what you did for me!! ⇒

01/05/2019

Letter from Heike Jürrens to the author, June 1998

Appreciation art sketch by Heike

A communication I later had with the lady I spoke with from the school in Germany further attested to how she and her colleagues were deeply touched by all the efforts that went into locating Heike and returning her wallet to her. She related that God's presence in this situation was evident by the manner in which people from faraway countries, different cultures, nationalities, and religions came together to help someone in need.

This is a story of the heart, the human heart at work in the spirit of goodwill toward another. It is the story of how a few people in the ordinary course of their lives and doing what they knew best came together from different cultures, nationalities, and human perspectives to return something valuable to someone they had never met. When done in the Spirit of Christ, Christian community is the natural result as God's all-sufficient grace has no limits. God sees the value in each of us and works through the people He puts in our lives to bring us back to Him.

Heike recently related to me that she had failed to mention something that happened when she returned to Germany. She visited her old school and was struck by her reception as almost a star. She was confused by it all until she learned from one of the teachers that Interpol had contacted the school about her. What a journey—from an Interstate access ramp on the outskirts of Florence, South Carolina, to an international police coordinating agency headquartered in Paris!

So we are left with a question: what proverbial road might you and I have been lost on, as that wallet was on that June day in 1998? And who might God in Christ Jesus have appointed or will appoint to be the person to stop along the way at some point in our lives and pick us up, as Tommy Coleman did with the wallet that day, sensing that something valuable had been lost? This may well have been your daybreak, that day when God made His way into your life or perhaps the daybreak that awaits you. God may well be working now in the silent, ordinary moments of your life, orchestrating the events to bring you back to Him, though you may not be consciously aware of it. But praise be to God that one day the time will come when you can look back on those times and say to yourself, "Ahh! God *was* there!"

EPILOGUE

"Do you love me?" Jesus asked (John 21:15, 16, 17). Perhaps the third time to hear this asked of me carried a message I had failed to grasp. *How many times will He ask this of me?* I wondered. *What is it He needs to hear from me?* Jesus laid down the stick He had been holding, moving closer to me as if to engage me in deeper conversation. By now, total daylight had filled the sky, warming our surroundings. The ground underneath where I had been seated created a slight discomfort in my back and legs. I adjusted my position, hoping to gain more comfort. I looked away momentarily, slightly intimidated by the stern gaze of Jesus, and then back at Him. I sensed there was more that Jesus wanted to help me understand. After a brief silence, Jesus looked directly into my eyes and said, "Consider the people I have put in your life, Paul, as a trusted servant of Mine. I have called you to feed them with My Word, to tend to them as the shepherd of a flock, to give yourself to them in ways that meet their spiritual and emotional needs. But what have you learned through them? Take note of what I have taught you and revealed to you through them and the many others I put in your life over the years. Paul, it is not always what you give them spiritually, how you encourage them, or the confidence you give them to press on with their lives. It is also a matter of what you learn from *them*, how I am using them to shape you into the person I have created you to be. Some have left your side, some are still with you, and others may be in faraway places. But each life carries within it a nugget of truth that you need for your spiritual edification. As you continue on your faith journey, Paul, lean over and pick up that nugget as if it is a stone lying in your path. Look at it, roll it around in your hand, feel the smooth surface, consider its size, its color, its shape. No two stones are the same, Paul. Like people, they all have their unique characteristics, but within them lay an element of truth that I will teach you. You cannot open that stone and see what is inside; only I can do that. So it is, Paul, with the people in your life. The truth is not what you see on the outside, only that which is inside, in their hearts. If you love me, Paul, you will feed and tend to my people. But you will also learn from those whom you least expect. Take this all to heart, Paul." I was so captivated by the words of Jesus that I lost all thought of my surroundings. His words were more intense, more direct.

He then asked me to do one more thing. "Close your eyes, Paul, and think deeply about what I have just said to you," Jesus said. "What is it that you need to know about My grace, My mercy, My peace, or My love that you have not come to experience? Meditate deeply on this, Paul."

For a couple of minutes, I heard nothing but the sounds of the elements—the waves quietly breaking upon the shore, the gentle rustling of the leaves from the grove of trees behind us, a cool breeze softly brushing against my face. *And then it happened.* I felt the comforting hand of Jesus resting on my right shoulder, and with words ever so soothing, He said to me, "Open your eyes, My child." I opened my eyes, looked up, and there before me and all around me stood ephemeral images of people Jesus had put in my life over the years. Some had left this world; others remained. Among them were my mom and dad, my grandfather Grampie from Massachusetts, aunts and uncles, former schoolteachers, Sunday school teachers, pastors, and friends who had been very much a part of my life.

An ineffable joy overtook me that words could not describe. I looked all around, trying to take it all in. Each one I looked on brought a multitude of memories. Soon, another strange manifestation caught my attention. Among the many recognizable faces stood several vague human figures, not at all recognizable. I gazed, squinting and trying as best I could to find some identifiable features, in hopes of recognizing them. My efforts were futile.

Having given me the time to experience this, Jesus then turned to me and said, "Paul, these whom you recognize are the people I have given you throughout your life to attend to you on your journey of faith; those who have been a godly example for you and have helped you understand who I am to and for you. The others whose faces you cannot distinguish are those I have yet to send to you. But you will know them when they come into your life, as I have more work to do in you. And I will do it through them. This will be My way of breaking into your life with another revealed truth I have for you."

So I conclude this book with a question, one I must continually ask myself and hopefully you will do likewise. Can I afford to treat casually the people God puts in my life, without understanding the redemptive value He brings to me through each of them? For every brother or sister in Christ shines in some way through the dark areas of my life, bringing forth rays of hope. And yes, as devoted followers of Jesus Christ, we know Christ as our Great Shepherd, and we know the green pastures in which He maketh us to lie down as the lush "fields" where we meet the very people through whom He teaches us faith lessons—granting us spiritual nourishment to press on with our lives. Every new understanding comes as the light of God's truth revealed in Jesus Christ. A daybreak, the dawning of a new and blessed day feeding and tending to us with the spiritual nourishment to sustain us on life's faith journey and paving the way to eternal life.

"Do you love Me?" Jesus asks.

"Come, then, and have breakfast. Afterward, we will journey on together."

AFTERWORD

Late one morning, I sat at the kitchen table, gazing out of the bay window at the street in front of our house. My eyes wavered between the outside surroundings and the computer screen in front of me. Wrestling with manuscript revisions is perhaps the most tedious and difficult task of the writing process, especially for me. *How can I clarify this point I am trying to make? How can I be more precise and succinct? What words or phrases can best elicit my emotions at a particular juncture in the story?* Revisions. Revisions. Revisions.

A few minutes later, Laura walked into the kitchen and asked, "Do you want to read the poem I just wrote?" Laura is a gifted poet and has written a hundred or more poems over the years. In recent weeks, she had been sending some of her previous writings to many of the elder members of our church. The response she received from some of these recipients had inspired her to continue writing and to broaden her mailing list. She handed me the poem, and I read it. I was amazed. She had not written the poem with my book in mind, only what she felt inspired to write at that time. What I read encapsulated all that I had tried to convey in my manuscript—how God puts people in our lives at various stages to mature us spiritually and to be conduits of God's blessings in Christ Jesus. Yes, thank You, Lord, for the people and for the love of a godly wife.

Thank You, Lord, for the People

Thank you, O Lord, for the people
You put in my life every day:
People to laugh with and play with,
Neighbors who would run and would play,
Friends who gave of themselves to me,
Spending with me precious time,
Friends who would travel to new places,
Together new mountains we'd climb.

All through my life are the angels
Who helped in my time of need.
They brought me great love and comfort,
Were faithful in word and in deed.
They taught me truth from the Bible
And helped me in learning to pray.
Some wiped my tears and calmed my fears
As I listened and learned to obey.

I wonder if I have done this
For others I've known in my life.
Did I ease their pain and sorrow?
Did I bring about less strife?
I pray I brought them peace and hope
And stayed with them for a while,
Not rushing off to leave them there,
And perhaps I made them smile.

O Lord, I'm ever grateful.
You've blessed my life with Your love
Through those who live with me on Earth
And through those in heaven above.
Your grace and mercy come to me

Each day as long as I live.
Thank You, Lord. I've felt your touch
Through people who were willing to give.[7]

Laura Gasque
1-10-19
Copyright 2019

ENDNOTES

1   Taken from notes of a personal journal entry dated December 27, 1992
2   *"Mere Christianity,"* by C.S. Lewis copyright C.S. Lewis Pte. Ltd. 1942, 1943, 1944, 1952, pages 158-159.
    Extract reprinted by permission.
3   Ibid., page 160.
4   Edwin Hatch, (words), *Breathe on Me, Breath of God,* Public Domain, The United Methodist Hymnal
    (Nashville, Tennessee: The United Methodist Publishing House, 1989); page 420,
5   I have attempted here to format the text exactly as it came to me from Willie on that day.
6   My opening statement from the manuscript of Willie's eulogy
7   Laura Gasque, "Thank You, Lord, for the People," Copyright 2019

CPSIA information can be obtained
at www.ICGtesting.com
Printed in the USA
BVHW031122110919
558046BV00024B/70/P

9 781973 670018